JOHN GARFIELD
His Life and Films

JOHN GARFIELD
His Life and Films

James N. Beaver, Jr.

South Brunswick and New York: A. S. Barnes and Company
London: Thomas Yoseloff Ltd

© 1978 by A. S. Barnes and Co., Inc.

A. S. Barnes and Co., Inc.
Cranbury, New Jersey 08512

Thomas Yoseloff Ltd
Magdalen House
136-148 Tooley Street
London SE1 2TT, England

Library of Congress Cataloging in Publication Data

Beaver, James N 1950-
John Garfield.

Includes index.
1. Garfield, John.
PN2287.G377B4 1977   791.43'028'0924   75-38450
ISBN 0-498-01890-3

Dedicated, with love, to

My father, *Norman Beaver,* whose dreams for me are becoming a slightly different reality

And to

My mother, *Dorothy Beaver,* who, in 1958, introduced me to my first John Garfield movie

Contents

Acknowledgments

For priceless aid in obtaining information and/or materials, I am indebted especially to David Garfield, and also to the Academy of Motion Picture Arts and Sciences, Joey Adams, the American Film Institute, Robert Blake, John Branscum, Don Bristow, Robert Brown, Joan Crawford, Central State University Library, Dallas Public Library, Bill Demand, B. D. Duncan (Duncan Posters), Dennis Fry, W. H. Crain and Joseph Neal (University of Texas Theatre Library), Ragan Haggard, Mike Johnson, Congressman John Jarman, Larry Edmunds Bookshop, Clifford McCarty, Dr. Arthur McClure, Ed Medard, Alvin Naifeh, University of Oklahoma Library, Gregory Peck, Abraham Polonsky, Ronald Reagan, Olle Rosberg, Bob and Charles Smith (Movie Poster Service), Jerry Wiedenkeller, Rolf Wickman, John Wooley, and above all, Susan Dalton of the Wisconsin Center for Theatre Research.

Also, I wish to thank for their unflagging encouragement: Tom Allard, Clay and Linda Barnes, Denise, Renee, and Teddlie Beaver, Marina Blevins, Lin Campbell, Cindy Carroll, Candy Couger, James Louie Edgin, Rick Gragg, Marilyn Harris, Alan, Ken, Ron, and Anne Keef, Billie Langley, Bob Linn, Candy Monday, Patrick Morey, Thelma Nixon, Don and Annette Pate, Dan Rasmussen, Sandy Shields, Rick Shields, Carl Silberman, Judge Springer, Judy Stephens, Greg Turner, Glenda Thompson, Gary Varner, Tim and Nancy West, Sandy Williams, Hank and Louise Worden, the Frontier City Gunfighters, and most of all, Bob Galey.

JOHN GARFIELD
His Life and Films

Part I
SAGA OF A GOLDEN BOY

"The Late John Garfield Blues" is an aptly titled song by John Prine that deals with the odd man out, the loser trying to stay alive in a hostile world. The title is fitting because, for the short fourteen years of Garfield's film career, he most frequently characterized outsiders struggling to survive without surrendering their principles. Instances of this theme occur in much of the world's great literature, Dumas, Hugo, and Thomas Wolfe creating prime examples of the man confused in a society seemingly set against him, confused by the tensions at work within his own soul. Garfield, to be sure, was not restricted to this type role. But a quick glance at some of his films reveals a strong similarity of shading in many of his parts, a similarity that began to grate on reviewers and audiences who wished to see Garfield's versatility explored to a greater extent.

Though his career was tragically short, Garfield's record figures well alongside those of his contemporaries, Bogart, Cagney, Raft, Robinson, Tracy, and Wayne. Among his thirty-five films are five Academy Award Winners in nineteen nominations, including two acting nominations for Garfield. He won one Best Actor award from the National Board of Review, which placed two of his pictures on its annual ten-best lists. Eight of his films were top-grossers for their years, and he won an Antoinette Perry award for his stage work. John Garfield was a major star, whose value at the box office compared favorably with that of his most popular co-stars: Bette Davis, Pat O'Brien, Edward G. Robinson, Lana Turner, Joan Crawford, Spencer Tracy, Jennifer Jones, and Cary Grant, among others. He gave us ample reason to wish his career had been longer, but there is no lament for what was. Garfield was an innovation among screen

actors when he first appeared, and he continued to inject a freshness into even the most pedestrian of roles, and an added brilliance into the good parts. Had he lived, he might conceivably have emerged as one of the two or three greatest actors of the screen. As it was, he achieved a level of excellence reached by few actors in many more years of work.

In the field of motion picture literature, from its beginnings through the mid-thirties, the protagonist was almost invariably a self-assured man, fighting only the forces of clear-cut evil in a black-and-white world. Gary Cooper, Errol Flynn,

Drawing by the author.

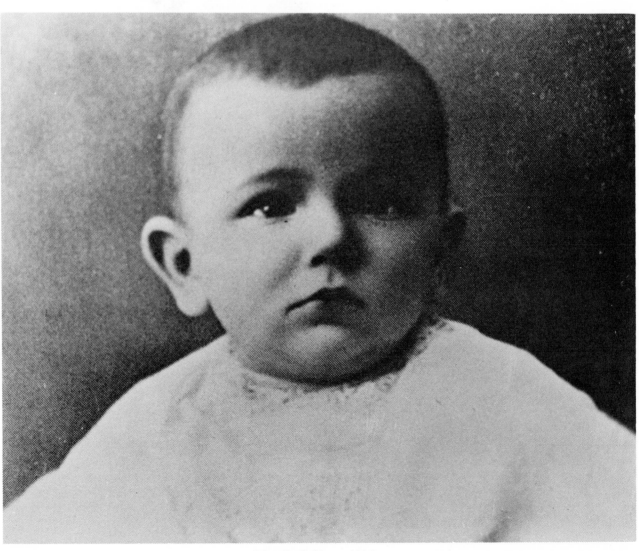

Jules Garfinkle, c. 1914.

Jules Garfinkle, 1917.

No matter how powerful the villainous forces, we knew that the hero's goodness would overcome, whether he knew or not.

In 1938, however, a new "hero" appeared on American theatre screens. This character was an amazing innovation, as far as motion pictures were concerned, and it is with difficulty today that we accept the fact that moviegoers almost forty years ago found his arrival startling. Here was a man, attractive for all his surly slovenliness, who felt little pride in himself and none in the society that had spawned him. He verged on paranoia in the fear and disgust he felt for "them," the unseen powers that were "out to get him." His stout insistence on fending for himself, coupled with his distaste for a steady job within the system, put him at odds, not only with contemporary society, but with his own cynical, yet basically decent, self. The film in which this rebellious hero first took shape was *Four Daughters.* The actor who portrayed him was John Garfield.

Garfield's youth is reminiscent of the first reel from any of his early films. He was born in the poverty of Rivington Street on New York's East Side on March 4, 1913. His parents, David and Hannah Garfinkle, named the boy Jules. David Garfinkle worked as a tailor and presser, while Hannah kept house and cared for Jules and his younger brother, Michael (known as "Max"). When Jules was seven, his mother died after a short illness. David Garfinkle remarried soon thereafter, taking Jules to live with him in the Bronx and leaving Max with an uncle in Brooklyn. Jules was left alone much of the time, his father being busy at his factory pressing job or at the local synagogue where he served as a cantor on weekends and holidays. Free to roam the streets, young Jules Garfinkle seemed headed on the road to delinquency. Infractions of the law were frequent, though he later stated that he and his friends "never robbed at gunpoint. Just stealing potatoes or apples from the market. But that's a poor boy, not a bad boy."

After one close scrape with the law, Jules was sent to Junior High School 45, a special school for problem children. Here he encountered the principal, Angelo Patri, the distinguished child psychologist, whose students have included poet Joy Davidman, sculptor John Amore, and scientist William Hassler. Shortly before his death in September, 1965, Patri spoke of his former pupil: "I

and Clark Gable were upright men, pitted against their exact opposites, solidly evil opponents such as Basil Rathbone, Akim Tamiroff, and Charles Laughton. We, the audience, accepted this blanket version of right and wrong, and we were asked to do no more. There was no questioning of motives. The motives simply existed, and no one asked why.

In 1926.

With high school drama class, 1928.

felt I needed to help Jules find an outlet for his abundant exuberance, and I thought that boxing might do the trick." Boxing meshed well with young Garfinkle's personality, and he progressed so well that he reached the semifinals in the New York Golden Gloves tournament. The experience he gained in this sport was to serve him well in later years.

Jules had suffered for several years from a bad stutter, and Patri took steps to alleviate this infirmity. He enrolled Jules in the school's elocution and drama classes. The boy excelled in this field as he had in boxing, and won the state oratorical contest held by the *New York Times* in 1927, with a speech entitled "Franklin, the Peacemaker of the Constitution." While in Junior High 45, Jules made his first stage appearance, as a spear-carrier in Shakespeare's *Julius Caesar*. His appetite for drama exceeded that for debate, and at the end of his junior high school years he wrote to the well-known Jewish actor Jacob Ben-Ami, asking "how a boy like me can get on the stage." Ben-Ami replied, suggesting that he try to enroll in the drama school run by the famed European actress Maria Ouspenskaya. Jules applied to the Ouspenskaya school, implying that Ben-Ami recommended a scholarship for him. He was accepted and attended there nights, working with directors such as Richard Boleslavsky, while going to classes at Textile High and Theodore Roosevelt High schools during the day.

Jules Garfinkle was fifteen in 1928, and that year Angelo Patri influenced the Heckscher Foundation to give the youth a scholarship to its drama school. Julie, as he was know to his friends then and throughout his life, sold newspapers for six dollars a week, and Patri contributed another five dollars weekly for his support. Years later, Garfield testified to working at this time as "a bit player with Fritz Lieber's Shakespearean players at a buck a throw," although his first job of which there is specific record was while with the Heckscher group. Jules appeared in their productions of *Lost Boy*, about life in a reformatory, and in *A Midsummer Night's Dream*. He also worked one summer acting and entertaining in a Vermont "Borscht Belt" summer camp.

Jules Garfinkle changed his name to Jules Garfield in 1932 and was accepted into Eva Le Galliene's Civic Repertory Theatre company. His first salaried part came in their Chicago production

of Elmer Rice's *Counsellor-at-Law,* with Otto Kruger in the lead. Early in 1932, Paul Muni, who had the lead in the New York production of the same play, left for California to fulfill a movie obligation. Otto Kruger took his place in the New York show, with Garfield and several others also taking parts in the Broadway production. When Muni returned in September of that year, Kruger returned to Chicago, but Garfield and the others remained with the New York cast, which included John Qualen and Ned Glass. The show, in which Garfield played a bit role, closed later that fall, and Jules left for California, intending to work his way cross-country with a friend.

The two boys first found jobs operating a tipple near the coal mines of Greensburg, Pennsylvania. They soon left the mines, making their ways west and finding work on the Kansas farm of a German couple named Stein. The Steins like Jules and offered to adopt him, but he still wanted to see California, and so declined their proposal.

A broad variety of jobs awaited the boys when they at last reached California. They harvested wheat, fought forest fires, washed dishes, picked fruit, waited tables at a tourist camp, drove trucks,

and worked for two months in the melon fields of Modesto Valley. While in California, nineteen-year-old Jules attempted to join the U.S. Marine Corps, but did not pass the physical examination. Contrary to a long-standing rumor, Garfield did *not* appear at this time in Warner's *Footlight Parade.* (See Appendix I.) On the return trip to New York, Garfield and his friend were arrested for vagrancy, and spent nine days in the Austin, Texas, jail.

Immediately upon his return to New York, Jules got a position with Macy's Department Store as a sales clerk. He soon saved enough money to marry Roberta Seidman, a girl he had known since high school. Soon after their marriage in 1932, he began rehearsals for the Civic Repertory Theatre production of *Peace on Earth,* by George Sklar and Albert Maltz (who was later to be one of the blacklisted screenwriters known as the Hollywood Ten). The play, directed by Robert Sinclair, opened at the Civic Repertory Theatre on November 29, 1933, with Garfield in a small part as a messenger. After one hundred twenty-six performances, it closed, reopening two weeks later at the Forty-fourth Street Theatre and running for

three weeks. In this second engagement, Garfield played "Bob Peters" in addition to his original role.

During the run of *Peace on Earth,* Garfield encountered Clifford Odets, a former neighbor in the Bronx, who had helped form the Group Theatre company in 1930-31 with Harold Clurman, Lee Strasberg, and Cheryl Crawford. The Group consisted of a number of socially conscious actors, directors, and playwrights who had banded together due to their disdain for the commercialism of the theater and to their general leftist leanings. Odets recommended Garfield to the Group, and Jules was taken on as an apprentice in Ellenville, New York, where the Group's plays were prepared for production. His first show with the company was Odets's *Waiting For Lefty,* in a small role as one of the striking cab-drivers. He followed this in November 1934 with a dual role in *Gold Eagle Guy,* by Melvin Levy, in which most of the cast, which included Odets, Elia Kazan, and Morris Carnovsky, played multiple parts. It ran for sixty-five performances.

Jules Garfield's best role with the Group Theatre came in February 1935. He was given a lead in Odets's play *Awake and Sing,* with other roles portrayed by Art Smith, Stella Adler, and Roman Bohnen. Harold Clurman directed the production, which ran for 209 performances. Garfield's reviews were good, and he followed the play with two more for the Group, *Weep for the Virgins* and *Johnny Johnson.*

In 1937, Garfield was offered the lead in Marc Connelly's production of Arthur Kobler's *Having Wonderful Time.* Critical comment was effusive, for Garfield in particular, and the play was included in Burns Mantle's Ten Best of the Year list. Nonetheless, it closed after thirty-two performances. This was due to an offer from Clifford Odets to Garfield for the lead in Odets's new play, *Golden Boy,* which the Group was producing. Garfield left his three-hundred-dollar-a-week role in *Having Wonderful Time* at Odets's insistence, only to find that Harold Clurman, the new play's director, had decided over Odets's objections to cast his brother-in-law, Luther Adler, in the lead role as the young violin-playing boxer. In Clurman's book about the Group, he explains this strange casting reversal: "Garfield was obviously the type, but he had neither the pathos nor the variety, in my opinion, to sustain the role."

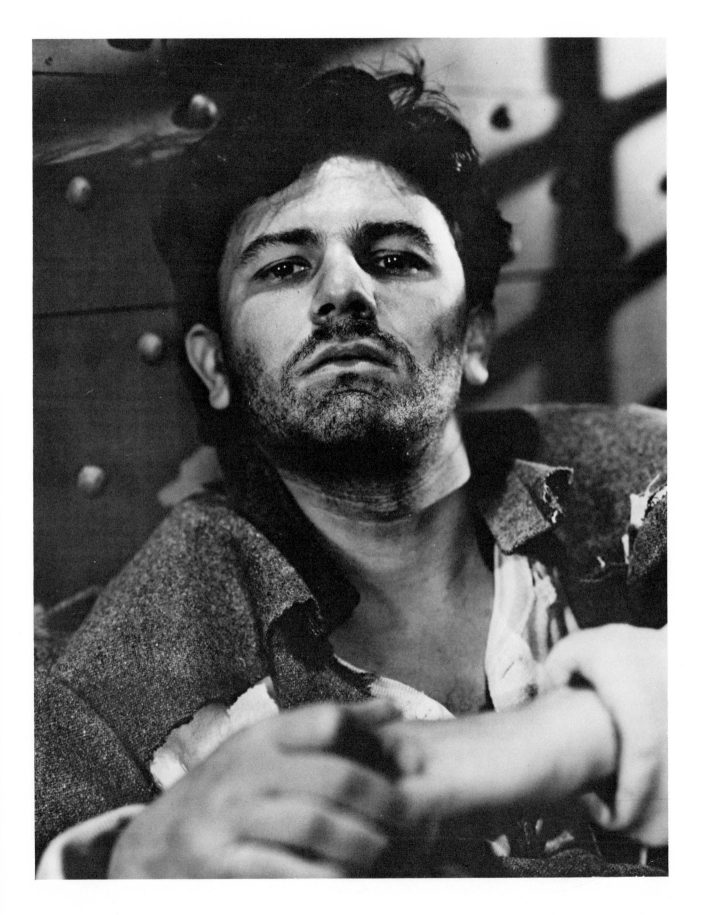

Instead, Clurman cast Garfield in the comedy role of Siggie, the cab driver, for which the actor received forty dollars and good reviews. Several years later, Garfield said of this period that "it seemed to me that in the Group lay the future of American drama." However, at the time, he became embittered at losing a part that many persons considered perfect for him, and with the encouragement of his wife, Robbie, he signed a seven-year contract with Warner Brothers studios, on the condition that he be allowed to do one play a year on sixty days' notice. Warners, who had been trying to sign Garfield for some time, was happy to comply. Of this media change he said, "I came to Hollywood fully expecting to hate it and

all set for the kick in the pants I felt sure I would get. In fact, when I signed with the studio I left a good, wide, neat and clean exit through which to make my farewell bow with as much grace as possible." However, this stage-clause was used only once in the next seven years.

Upon his arrival in California, Jules was informed of his new screen name, John Garfield. Story has it that Warner executives were reluctant to let him keep even his surname, until one of them remembered a President of the United States named Garfield. "And remember, they shot him," the actor later quipped. His first film for Warners was *Four Daughters*. Released in mid-1938, the film received immediate acclaim, most of it for

With Claude Rains, Paul Muni, Edward G. Robinson, Mr. Hornblow (Myrna Loy's husband), Mrs. Melvyn Douglas, Gloria Stuart, James Cagney, Groucho Marx, Aline MacMahon, Henry Fonda, Gale Sondergaard, Myrna Loy, Melvyn Douglas, Carl Laemmle signing petition urging economic break with Nazi Germany, 1938.

24

Garfield's portrayal of the down-and-out composer, Mickey Borden. He won the National Board of Review Best Actor award, and was nominated for a Best Supporting Actor Oscar. He was hailed as the top new star of 1938, and the old platitude of "overnight success" was dusted off and applied once more.

Immediately after the release and success of *Four Daughters,* the Group Theatre apparently realized their loss and offered Garfield the lead in their London production of *Golden Boy,* which he rather understandably refused. Harry Cohn of Columbia studios also wanted Garfield for the film version of *Golden Boy,* but Jack Warner was at odds with Cohn and refused the trade. The role was a success for a newcomer named William Holden, in his first film. About this time, Garfield and his wife had their first child, a daughter, whom they named Katherine.

With the success of *Four Daughters,* Warner Brothers rushed their new star into as many films as possible, most of them about characters strangely similar to Mickey Borden. Garfield even played Borden again, in a flashback sequence in *Four Wives,* the first of several *Daughters* sequels. He was scheduled to make *Each Dawn I Die,* but due to availability problems it eventually starred James Cagney and George Raft. He made five pictures in 1939, including *Blackwell's Island, They Made Me a Criminal,* and *Juarez. Criminal* was a nonmusical Busby Berkeley programmer, and *Juarez* featured Garfield as Mexican revolutionary Porfirio Diaz, a role performed on Broadway by Edward G. Robinson. He was suspended for the first of ten times for refusing to play any more roles like "that snotty fisherman" in *Daughters Courageous,* an unofficial remake of *Four Daughters.* In an interview with Bosley Crowther at

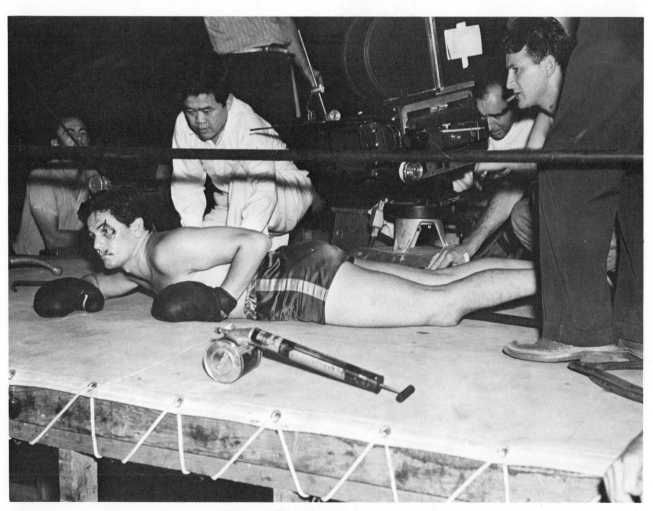

Shooting They Made Me a Criminal, *1938.*

During Juarez *shooting, 1938.*

After completing *Castle on the Hudson* (another remake of *20,000 Years in Sing Sing*) in 1940, Garfield exercised his one-play-a-year clause for the only time in his contract run. He returned to Braodway for the National Theatre production of Albert Bein's *Heavenly Express,* which featured Aline MacMahon, Harry Carey, and Jack Lambert. Garfield played the Overland Kid in this fantasy about a train that takes dead tramps to hobo paradise. The play received fair reviews, although there were good notices for Garfield and Carey. Burns Mantle waxed enthusiastic about Garfield's performance, but Sidney Whipple of the *New York World-Telegram* thought that the actor played the role as "a sort of overgrown Peter Pan, with over-much leaping about." The play closed after only twenty performances. Miss MacMahon's

this time, Garfield said, "If an actor doesn't have a point of view, he doesn't make a dent. And I mean to make a dent." This philosophy was to remain with him throughout his career, sometimes at a hazard to that career.

At the "Dodge City" publicity festivities with (on platform) Frances Robinson, Lya Lys, Alan Hale, Gloria Dickson, Jane Wyman, Gilbert Roland, John Payne, (standing) Frank McHugh, Chief Santa Fe, Maxie Rosenbloom, Priscilla Lane, Lee Lyles, Errol Flynn, Jack Warner, Rosemary Lane, Humphrey Bogart, Wayne Morris, (kneeling) Leon Turrou, Hoot Gibson, Ann Sheridan, Buck Jones, Guinn Williams, Olivia deHavilland, 1939.

mother, in consolation, wrote to her: "I think the reviews are very good for you. I guess the high moguls here resent John Garfield's leaving the pictures for a play. And they give little digs about him every so often. But they can't take away his talent anymore than yours!" Garfield returned to Hollywood, completing three more films in 1940.

With Francis Lederer, Robbie Garfield at 1939 premiere.

With Errol Flynn, 1941.

Oil pictures were big that year, and Warners rushed their remake of *Flowing Gold,* with Garfield and Pat O'Brien, into release in order to beat MGM's *Boom Town.*

Jack London's *The Sea Wolf* was Garfield's first film of 1941. He was a great London fan, and suffered two bitter disappointments when Warner Brothers refused to loan him to Columbia for the film of London's novel *The Adventures of Martin Eden* (1942) or to United Artists in 1943 for *Jack London.* Those roles went to Glenn Ford and Michael O'Shea, respectively. Garfield followed *The Sea Wolf* with a gangster melodrama, *Out of the Fog.*

With the beginning of World War II in 1941, Garfield was one of the few leading men to sustain his career throughout the war. He did, however, fight the Nazis on film in *Dangerously They Live,* the Japanese in *Air Force,* and Spanish fascists in RKO's *The Fallen Sparrow.* Garfield's second child, a son, was born in 1942, and named David Patton. (David grew up to become an actor, appearing in several films, *The Swimmer, MacKenna's Gold,* and *That Cold Day in the Park* among them, and on the New York stage.) In 1944, Garfield toured Italy entertaining the troops and while there, made a secret trip behind Yugoslavian lines to do a show for a group of partisans. This trip was to be the indirect cause of some problems for Garfield a few years later. Upon his return from Italy, he stated, "This foxhole circuit is an eye-opener in every way. Hollywood war

With Jean Gabin at the Hollywood Canteen, 1942.

With Jean Darling, Sheila Rogers, and troops in Italy, 1944.

movies were never like this." In 1941, he had led the first group of entertainers on a tour of military bases in the Caribbean. The tour, which included Ray Bolger, Chico Marx, Mitzi Mayfair, Jane Pickens, and Laurel and Hardy, so influenced Garfield that he produced an article (actually ghosted by Al Leavitt) for *Theatre Arts,* encouraging other performers to make similar trips. During his Italian tour, Garfield had received his draft notice. Returning home and reporting for induction, he was told to "go home. You're too old and you've got two kids."

The New York Times announced in 1943 that Maxwell Anderson wanted John Garfield for his new play, *Storm Operation,* and that Garfield was interested. However, like his plans in 1938 to

With Jack Warner, Joy Page, 1943.

return to New York for the Group production of *The Silent City,* nothing came of the proposal, and Garfield remained in Hollywood, making such films as *Destination Tokyo, Between Two Worlds,* and *Hollywood Canteen.* This last picture was about the worthy club for servicemen, which Garfield had co-founded with Bette Davis.

Roberta Garfield and her husband had unofficially separated in 1943. In late 1945, while on a picnic with her father's secretary, their daughter Katherine developed a sore throat and died a few hours later of what was later termed a streptococcal infection (strep throat). As a result of her

With Eleanor Roosevelt, Red Skelton, Lucille Ball at White House birthday party for the First Lady, 1944.

death, the Garfields reconciled, and on January 10, 1946, their daughter Julie was born.

Theater marquees in the mid-forties glowed with John Garfield's name above titles like *The Pride of the Marines* and *The Postman Always Rings Twice.* His last film on his Warner contract, *Humoresque,* was completed in early 1946, and immediately he began a revival of Clifford Odets's *Awake and Sing* fo the Hollywood Actors' Laboratory, in the role originally performed by Luther Adler. Alfred Ryder played Garfield's original part of Ralph Berger. Warner Brothers offered him a new fifteen-year contract at two hundred thousand dollars per year, which Garfield refused in order to free-lance and to form his own studio, Enterprise Studios. His first film for his own company was *Body and Soul,* which won many awards and

Gathering signatures for a petition to Congress urging price and rent controls, July 1946.

Talking with co-stars Leon Ames and Cecil Kellaway between scenes of The Postman Always Rings Twice, 1946.

With David Niven and Lili Palmer on the set of Body and Soul, *1947.*

Garfield put it, "because I couldn't see eye to eye with the producers." In fact, the only one of the projects to be realized was *Gentleman's Agreement.* Garfield had only a twenty-minute appearance, about which he said, "They hesitated to offer me the part. They said I was a star and this was not a star's part." The film was very well received, winning that year's Best Picture Academy Award. Gregory Peck won a Best Actor nomination (in competition with Garfield's *Body and Soul* nomination), but also lost to Colman. Garfield later said of his role, "That was a part I didn't act. I felt it with all my heart."

garnered for Garfield his first Oscar nomination in the Best Actor category. He lost the award, however, to Ronald Colman for that actor's bravura performance in *A Double Life.*

Garfield recorded a Decca children's album in 1947, entitled *Herman the Ermine in Rabbit Town,* and in May, he announced plans to do films of Thomas Wolfe's *Look Homeward, Angel,* Laura Z. Hobson's *Gentleman's Agreement, Volpone* (with Charles Laughton as Volpone and himself as the valet, Mosca), and Theodore Strauss's novel *Moonrise.* The *Moonrise* project fell through, as

Clowning with Marie Windsor, 1947.

With Tommy Dorsey, 1947.

The House Un-American Activities Committee investigation of Hollywood Communist organizations began in 1947, leading to the studio blacklist and imprisonment of the Hollywood Ten (ten well-known directors and writers who had refused Congressional questioning. They included Alvah Bessie, Edward Dmytryk, Ring Lardner, Jr., Albert Maltz, Dalton Trumbo, Herbert Biberman, Lester

Cole, John Howard Lawson, Samuel Ornitz, and Adrian Scott). An organization called the "Committee for the First Amendment," founded by John Huston, William Wyler, and Phillip Dunne, circulated an *amicus curiae* petition on the Ten's behalf, stressing the right of Americans to refuse questioning. Garfield signed it. He had been quoted that May in *Motion Picture* magazine as saying, "Actors should express their political convictions."

In the winter of 1947, Garfield again traveled to New York, this time to play the lead in Jan de Hartog's *Skipper Next To God.* This production by the nonprofit Experimental Theatre paid Garfield eighty dollars a week. Of his return to Broadway he said, "Screen acting is my business. But I get my kicks on Broadway." In order to participate in *Skipper,* he turned down the role of Stanley Kowalski in Tennessee Williams's *Streetcar Named Desire,* a role which went to a young Nebraskan named Marlon Brando. Garfield reasoned at the time that the role of Blanche would overshadow that of Stanley, but also stated, "I wanted to do *Skipper,* because it is the story of a man and his conscience. A story of a man who has to make

decisions." For his performance in *Skipper Next To God*, Garfield won a 1948 Tony Award. He was also recipient of the first La Guardia Award from the Non-Sectarian Anti-Nazi League, and the East Side Scroll of Honor from Madison House, a New York settlement house, for the humanitarian aspects of his roles in *Skipper* and *Gentleman's Agreement*. On the same day that he received these awards, Garfield was "roasted" by his good friend Milton Berle and other members of the Friar's Club. A member of the Executive Board of the Screen Actors Guild, and of the Independent Citizens' Committee of Arts, Sciences, and Professions, Garfield was quoted at this time as saying, "I'm a fighting liberal, a progressive. Only Hollywood has made me a little lazy, a little complacent."

Upon Garfield's return to Hollywood, a *Look* interview listed his hobbies as playing tennis with Peter Lorre, and a weekly poker game at the Hoyle Club with George S. Kaufman, Russell Crouse, Franklin P. Adams, and Ira Gershwin. The article also announced Garfield's plans to film a biography

With Phyllis Thaxter.

of Angelo Patri and to "play Romeo with guts." His next picture, however, was *Force of Evil,* the first film directed by Abraham Polonsky, who had written *Body and Soul.* It was also the last film Polonsky directed before the unofficial Hollywood blacklist that prevented Polonsky, Anne Revere, Gale Sondergaard, Michael Wilson, and others from working anywhere in the film industry, due to alleged Communist connections.

John Garfield next appeared on the screen in *We Were Strangers,* a melodrama for which he and director John Huston intended to screen-test a new young actress. The test never came about, because producer S. P. Eagle got wind of it and insisted that Garfield and Huston pay for it themselves. The actress, a stunning blonde named Marilyn Monroe, did not get the part.

Garfield next returned to New York, opening in February 1949 in Clifford Odets's play *The Big Knife,* at the National Theatre. The play, which ran for three months, garnered poor-to-fair reviews, although Garfield himself received excellent notices. Howard Barnes in the *New York Herald-Tribune* called Garfield's performance "genuine artistry," and the *New York Sun* lauded him for contributing more to the character than the playwright had done. While in New York, he did an unbilled bit as a loafer in Fletcher Markle's film *Jigsaw.* Henry Fonda, Marlene Dietrich, and others also played cameo roles.

In June of that year, Garfield was cited in an FBI report from a confidential informer read at the espionage trial of Judith Coplon as having been "singled out for praise" in a German-language publication of the Moscow-dominated Comintern. The same day, the California State Senate Committe on Un-American Activities listed Garfield as one of several hundred prominent individuals who 'followed or appeased some of the Communist Party line program over a long period of time." The list, which included virtually every film personality but John Wayne and Francis the Talking Mule, also gave the names of Edward G. Robinson, Gregory Peck, Mr. and Mrs. Fredric March, and Katharine Hepburn.

After shooting *Under My Skin* and narrating an Italian film, *Difficult Years,* in early 1950, Garfield announced plans to produce a film about a young protégé of composer Arturo Toscanini, with Toscanini appearing in the picture. Again his proposal fell through, and Garfield made another

With wife, Robbie, and children, David and Julie, 1950.

With Patricia Neal.

36

With wife and daughter, c. 1951.

film for someone else, this time a reworking of Hemingway's *To Have and Have Not,* Warner Brothers' *The Breaking Point.* An excellent film, Garfield said of it that he thought it was better than *Body and Soul.* Immediately after filming, Garfield joined Mildred Dunnock, Karl Malden, and Nehemiah Persoff in the ANTA production of Paul Green's adaptation of Ibsen's *Peer Gynt.* Opening in New York in January 1951, it ran for thirty-two performances.

Following *Peer Gynt,* John Garfield made what was to be his final film, *He Ran All the Way.* After completing this *film noir,* but before its release, Garfield was subpoenaed, on March 7, 1951, by the House Un-American Activities Committee. Also receiving subpoenas at this time were Anne Revere, Jose Ferrer, and Sterling Hayden. When

informed of the summons, Garfield told reporters, "I have nothing to hide. Perhaps they want some information from me since I served on the board of the Screen Actors Guild along with Miss Revere. I have always hated communism. It is a tyranny which threatens our country and the peace of the world. Of course then, I have never been a member of the Communist Party or a sympathizer with any of its doctrines. I will be pleased to cooperate with the committee."

Accompanied by his attorneys, Louis Nizer and Sidney Davis, Garfield traveled to Washington, where he testified for more than three hours on April 23. Among the questions he faced was one dealing with his secret performance in 1944 for Yugoslav partisans. The year after the war ended, the Yugoslav commander had visited Garfield in

With Phyllis Thaxter.

With Robbie, c. 1951.

Hollywood, and the actor had donated fifty dollars to help Yugoslav Relief. Soon thereafter, Garfield's name was linked to a Communist front, the American Committee for Yugoslav Relief. The House Committee was curious about his connec-

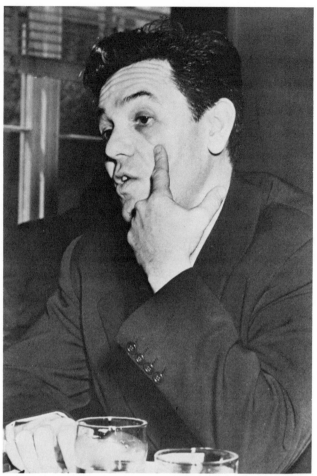

Testifying before HUAC, 1951.

Testifying before HUAC, April 1951.

tion with this front, but apparently accepted his explanation.

Concerning his signing of the *amicus curiae* brief in 1948 on behalf of the Hollywood Ten, Garfield stated that he had been asked to sign by a member of the Beverly Hills Tennis Club, possibly George Willner, who was later identified by HUAC as a "functionary in several prominent Communist Party organizations." But Garfield continually insisted that he was not certain who had asked him. The committee then inquired whether he would have signed it "if just anybody had walked up and asked you to." His reply: "Not if it was any stranger, no." The relationship that the *amicus curiae* bore to the Communist Party was never made clear, although the implication was that anyone who opposed the Committee was suspect, regardless of political affiliation. Sometimes committee members resorted to near-insults. When Garfield brought up a bad review he had received in the Communist *Daily Worker,* Representative Donald L. Jackson shot back: "The witness should know that this committee also shared the criticism of the *Daily Worker.*"

Garfield, in his testimony, also denied membership in the National Council of Arts, Sciences, and Professions (NCASP), an organization suspected of pro-Communist leanings. The committee attempted to prove his membership by showing him a 1948 clipping from the *Daily Worker* which stated that he had signed a statement from NCASP urging the abolition of HUAC, an attempt that seems somewhat irrational, considering the fact that many non-NCASP-members had also signed the statement. The committee also accused Garfield of attending a meeting of Russians at which a Russian film was shown. As it turned out, the meeting was actually a party given for a visiting Russian by the State Department, and the film was *The Bear,* a story written by Anton Chekhov in 1870.

Testifying before HUAC, 1951.

Garfield staunchly denied any Party connections, saying, "I'm no Red, no Pink, no fellow-traveler. I'd run like hell before lending my name knowingly to such a group. I am a Democrat by politics, a liberal by inclination, and a loyal citizen of this country by every act of my life." He added that he felt Communism should be outlawed, "to protect liberals like me."

Reactions to Garfield's testimony were mixed, within and without the House Committee. Representative Jackson told Garfield, "I am not entirely convinced of the whole accuracy and cooperation you are giving this committee. For one who is as intelligent and as well established as this witness has proven himself to be, it shows a naive or unintelligent approach to this problem for him to have lived with this activity ten, eleven, or fifteen years and not know more about it than this witness knows." Representative Morgan M. Moulder stated, however, "that nothing has been presented by this committee which associates you with the Communist Party," adding that he was convinced that Garfield was a "thoroughly and intensely loyal American citizen," and complimenting the actor for his "vigilant fight against Communism." The majority of the press showed faith in Garfield's statements, although some thought that a few obvious contradictions presented Garfield in a rather unfavorable light.

Twenty-five days after the committee hearing, HUAC sent Garfield's testimony to the Justice Department for comparison with FBI investigation records. This show of doubt by the Committee was a major jolt to Garfield and to his career, for, up until this time, journalistic and public opinion had been heavily with him. For the next ten months, he was unable to obtain a role in films or theatre.

Ronald Reagan, in his autobiography, *Where's the Rest of Me?,* recalls an incident in the late forties when he and William Holden had infiltrated a pro-Communist meeting in Beverly Hills. At the meeting, Reagan obtained the floor and attempted to explain facts that would have prevented the Red-sympathizers from "brainwashing" and using for their own ends several well-known and innocent people present. Greeted with boos and cat-calls, Reagan was rescued by John Garfield, a surprising fact, Reagan recalls, considering Garfield's usual opposition to Reagan. After Garfield's attempt to quiet the group with "Why don't you listen to him? He does have information

With children, 1952.

you don't have," Reagan states that he "saw a well-known character actor take John to the back of the garden. I could see him back John up against a tree and, with one hand holding him by the shirt front, he read an angry riot act, punctuated by a jabbing finger. John stayed back there, leaning against the tree, hands deep in his pockets, after the actor left him, and finally edged his way to a back gate and left."

Several of Garfield's friends and fellow film-workers voluntarily admitted their Communist Party connections, among them Clifford Odets, Elia Kazan, Robert Rossen, Budd Schulberg, and Sterling Hayden. But the facts concerning the Reagan incident, as well as the truth about Garfield's political environment, were to remain shrouded from public knowledge until after his death.

In March 1952, John Garfield obtained his first role since the House-ordered FBI investigation. It was also his last. In it, Garfield at long last played the part he was to have played fourteen years earlier. The ANTA revival of Clifford Odets's *Golden Boy* opened March 12, 1952, with Garfield in the lead as Joe Bonaparte. The cast, which included Lee J. Cobb, Jack Warden, and Jack Klugman, received excellent notices, though none more laudatory than those for Garfield. Richard Watts, Jr., of the *New York Post,* stated, "Luther Adler, in the original company, wasn't nearly as real, incisive, or moving as John Garfield is in the present production. Indeed, this strikes me as one of the finest performances that I have ever seen Mr. Garfield give, and it serves to remind us once more that, provided with the proper sort of role, he is one of the most brilliant and satisfying of American actors."

Following the success of *Golden Boy,* Garfield began efforts to reorder his life. He worked for several weeks with Arnold Foster of the Anti-Defamation League on a statement for the House Committee. He went over his previous testimony discrepancies and admitted lying to the committee. Stating that he had never been an official member of the Communist Party, adding that he was "more useful to them the other way," he went on to describe how an "emotional and sentimental" Hollywood actor could be drawn into the Party line program. Admitting membership in thirty-two front organizations and signing forty-two petitions, he also mentioned one attempt at breaking away

(the Ronald Reagan incident), and being forced back into line. He told of fourteen years of terror and fear in which he was approached by gunmen and his family was threatened. Realizing the jeopardy from both sides in which he was placing himself, Garfield courageously insisted upon re-vealing all the facts. Although the statement was never finished, the world has come to realize how hundreds of film people like Garfield donated their names and money to supposedly charitable Ameri-can organizations without having even a small part of the time necessary to fully investigate each one, and found themselves later listed as Party "sup-porters" unable to back out. During this period, Garfield also wrote a letter to Spyros Skouras, then head of Twentieth Century-Fox studios, asking for the lead role in *Taxi,* a part he desperately wanted. The role eventually went to Dan Dailey. Garfield also began a magazine article refuting Communism.

Rumor has it that Garfield quarreled with his wife, Roberta, over his political situation at this time. At any rate, in early May 1952, he moved out of their home at 88 Central Park West, and took a room at the Warwick Hotel, also in New

Iris Whitney, in whose apartment Garfield died.

York. On May 20th, following dinner at Luchow's Restaurant with actress Iris Whitney, Garfield returned with Miss Whitney to her apartment at 3 Gramercy Park. He complained of feeling ill shortly after arriving, but refused to allow her to call a doctor. He went to bed in her bedroom while she slept on a couch in the living room. In the morning, she was unable to awaken Garfield, and called Dr. Charles H. Nammack. At nine A.M., May 21, 1952, John Garfield was pronounced dead of a coronary thrombosis. The police report stated that there was nothing suspicious about Garfield's death. There is an existing story that Garfield had suffered a heart attack in 1949 due to playing fifty consecutive tennis matches on a bet, although this tale has that peculiar ring of truth most often found in fan magazines. The story may have arisen because of a book by Jay Kennedy, called *Prince Bart*. Published not long after Garfield's death, it resembles his life enough for it to be called fictionalization by some, cheap exploitation by others. Its hero, Bart Blaine, aware of a bad heart, commits suicide by playing a rugged tennis match in blistering heat. Whatever the case, Garfield had suffered mild heart attacks in 1949 and 1951, and had been warned by his doctors to "take it easy." The Communist Party immediately announced that his fatal attack had been the result of HUAC persecution. Garfield's will left an estate of one hundred-thousand dollars to his wife and two children.

At 2:15 P.M. on Friday, May 23, funeral services for John Garfield were held at Riverside Memorial Chapel in New York. Six hundred people filled the chapel to capacity, while ten thousand more crammed the streets outside. The *New York Times* called it "the largest turn-out for a funeral since that of Rudolph Valentino in 1926." Burial was in Westchester Hills Cemetery in Mount Hope, New York. That same day, Garfield's name was linked with yet another organization. In the *New York Times* obituary column appeared this notice: "Grand Street Boys Association sorrowfully announces the death of its beloved member, John Garfield."

John Garfield epitomized the ideology of the common man for Depression and post-Depression America. He was not the shining knight or white-hatted marshal in his films, but the idol with feet of clay that was so much nearer to mankind's reality. In the weaknesses of his characters, he showed us our own faults, and in the strengths of his characters, he gave us a road out of our faults. His films were often despairing in nature, but they also often gave us a hope of triumph, which in actuality is the triumph itself. He was the loser who, in his final understanding, won out after all. Although no "cult" of followers has sprung up such as that for Humphrey Bogart (however, one is showing signs of beginning), the legacy Garfield left is nonetheless real and valuable. The Garfield heritage can still be seen, not only in his films, but also in the roles played by such actors as Marlon Brando, Montgomery Clift, Steve McQueen, Robert Blake, and Paul Newman. They are the runners who carry the torch lit by John Garfield. His endowment to his profession can also be observed in the fact that his children, Julie and David, are working in the field their father loved so much.

In his eulogy for Garfield, Rev. Dr. Louis I.

David Garfield.

Julie Garfield.

44

Newman said, "John Garfield was a superbly endowed man who was gallant, lovable, and had a charm and personality that has made him almost an American legend. He was not an ordinary person, but he was unique and a sincere and genuine soul. His true nature showed through the masks he was asked to assume on the stage or in motion pictures. In his less than four decades, he lived a life of vivid experience and he gained critical recognition and the plaudits of his generation."

It might be added that John Garfield also gained the love of a people that knew him and felt a kinship to him, and whom he knew intimately and loved deeply.

Part II
THE FILMS

1
Four Daughters
1938

Credits:

A Warner Bros.-First National Picture. Directed by Michael Curtiz. Produced by Hal B. Wallis. Associate producers, Benjamin Glazer and Henry Blanke. Screenplay by Julius J. Epstein and Leonore Coffee. Based on a story by Fannie Hurst. Director of photography, Ernest Haller. Music by Max Steiner. Film editor, Ralph Dawson. Dialogue director, Irving Rapper. Assistant director, Sherry Shourds. Art director, John Hughes. Gowns by Orry-Kelly. Sound recorder, Stanley Jones. Music director, Leo F. Forbstein. Unit manager, Al Alleborn. Running time, 90 minutes.

Cast:

Adam Lemp	Claude Rains
Ann Lemp	Priscilla Lane
Kay Lemp	Rosemary Lane
Thea Lemp	Lola Lane
Emma Lemp	Gale Page
Mickey Borden	John Garfield
Felix Deitz	Jeffrey Lynn
Ben Crowley	Frank McHugh
Aunt Etta	May Robson
Ernest Talbot	Dick Foran
Mrs. Ridgefield	Vera Lewis
Jake	Tom Dugan
Sam	Eddie Acuff
Earl	Donald Kerr

Synopsis:

Musician Adam Lemp lives with his four equally musical daughters, Emma, Ann, Kay, and Thea. Ben Crowley and Ernest Talbot are the respective beaux of Thea and Emma, and Ann discovers a new admirer in Felix Deitz, a struggling young composer, who captures the affection of all the girls.

Just as Ann's interest in Felix begins to grow, he brings his orchestrator, Mickey Borden, around for a visit. Borden is a slovenly, cynical, mad-at-the-world young man who talks with a cigarette dangling from his mouth, refuses to be polite, and manages, with ease, to create a bad impression upon everyone. Ann immediately sets out to make him over, meanwhile accepting Felix's marriage proposal. However, Ann discovers that Emma loves Felix, and on her wedding day elopes instead with Mickey. Thea marries Ben soon thereafter. Emma realizes that she actually loves Ernest, and Ann struggles in poverty with Mickey. They are all reunited at Christmas. Mickey drives Felix to his train afterwards, realizing that Ann still loves and needs Felix. To clear the way for her, Mickey wrecks the car and dies. Felix returns, and together they mourn a man worth much more than he himself had believed.

Reviews:

Philip T. Hartung in *Commonweal:*

"The cast is good, and John Garfield is perfect as the unhappy fellow who expects a lightning bolt to catch up with him sooner or later. His appearance is a startling as would be that of a Hemingway character in a book by Jane Austen."

Newsweek:

"John Garfield steals the acting honors with his realistic protrayal of doomed pessimism . . . . [He] is undoubtably the outstanding film find of the year."

Time:

"In *Four Daughters'* almost negative cast, he [Garfield] is the sole positive charge."

B.R. Crisler in the *New York Times:*

'Four Daughters' is one of the best pictures of anyone's career, if only for the sake of the marvelously meaningful character of Mickey Borden as portrayed by John (formerly Jules) Garfield, who bites off his lines with a delivery so eloquent that we still aren't sure whether it is the dialogue or Mr. Garfield who is so bitterly brilliant. . . . Mr. Garfield is such a sweet relief from conventional screen types . . . that we can't thank Warner Brothers . . . enough for him."

Notes:

Four Daughters was nominated for five Academy Awards, including Best Picture and John Garfield for Best Supporting Actor. Garfield lost to Walter Brennan for *Kentucky,* but won the National Board of Review's Best Actor Award. Of the role, Garfield said, "Mickey Borden is foolproof and actor-proof. Getting the part was pure unadulterated luck and don't think for a minute that I ever kidded myself into thinking anything else." The film was remade as the musical *Young at Heart* ('54), with Frank Sinatra and Doris Day in the Garfield-Priscilla Lane roles. Coincidentally, Sinatra was also to play in *The Man With the Golden Arm* ('55) and *Suddenly* ('54), in the roles originally prepared with Garfield in mind.

Four Daughters opened at Radio City Music Hall in New York on August 9, 1938.

With Priscilla Lane and May Robson.

With Priscilla Lane.

With Priscilla Lane.

With Priscilla Lane.

With Priscilla Lane.

With Priscilla Lane.

With Priscilla Lane.

2
They Made Me a Criminal

1939

Credits:

A Warner Bros.-First National Picture. Directed by Busby Berkeley. Produced by Jack L. Warner and Hal B. Wallis. Associate producer, Benjamin Glazer. Screenplay by Sig Herzig. Based on a novel by Bertram Millhauser and Beulah Marie Dix. Director of photography, James Wong Howe. Music by Max Steiner. Film editor, Jack Killifer. Assistant director, Russ Saunders. Art director, Anton Grot. Costumes by Milo Anderson. Sound recorder, Oliver S. Garretson. Orchestrations by Leo F. Forbstein. Running time, 92 minutes.

Cast:

Johnnie	John Garfield
Tommy	Billy Halop
Angel	Bobby Jordan
Spit	Leo Gorcey
Dippy	Huntz Hall
T.B.	Gabriel Dell
Milt	Bernard Punsley
Detective Phelan	Claude Rains
Goldie	Ann Sheridan
Grandma	May Robson
Peggy	Gloria Dickson
Doc Ward	Robert Gleckler
Magee	John Ridgely
Budgie	Barbara Pepper
Ennis	William Davidson
Lenihan	Ward Bond
Malvin	Robert Strange
Smith	Louis Jean Heydt
J. Douglas Williamson	Ronald Sinclair
Rutchek	Frank Riggi
Manager	Cliff Clarke
Colucci	Dick Wessel
Sheriff	Raymond Brown
Speed	Irving Bacon
Splash	Sam McDaniel

Synopsis:

Johnnie, a prizefighter with obvious underworld connections, is involved in a murder, and, unable to prove his innocence, he quits boxing and flees to Arizona. Once there, he obtains work at a fruit ranch run by a kindly woman known as Grandma. The ranch is worked by a group of delinquent boys for whom Grandma provides a home. Johnnie teaches the boys to box, and begins to gentle under the influence of the old woman and her daughter. Peggy.

One day the boys go swimming in a water tank in the orange groves. As the tank is drained for irrigation, the water level drops so low that the boys cannot escape and they face drowning in the smooth-sided tank. Johnnie hears their cries, however, and rescues them. When Grandma is faced with eviction, Johnnie returns to the ring to win prize money to redeem the farm. Detective Phelan, who has trailed Johnnie from New York, sees the fight and prepares to arrest Johnnie. Before doing so, however, Phelan sees Johnnie's rehabilitation and drops the case. Wishing Johnnie luck, Phelan reports that he has been unable to find him.

Reviews:

Philip T. Hartung in *Commonweal:*

"Criminals and criminology dominate the screen offerings this week and 'They Made Me a Criminal' is the best of the group — because of John Garfield's superb performance as the tough, hard-hitting 'southpaw' who is forced to flee from a murder that is wrongly blamed on him."

Otis Ferguson in *The New Republic:*

"Garfield and the kids and the gal, the director and those who worried the script into shape — and even Claude Rains as the broken but hopeful flatfoot — these people manage to salvage enough truth out of it to make most of the business convincing and pleasant."

Newsweek:

"The role of Johnnie, a world's champion welterweight with a full set of vices, is tailor-made for Garfield. His brilliant characterization in a familiar role will serve as an exciting reminder that another East Side New Yorker is on his way to screen stardom."

B. R. Crisler in the *New York Times:*

"So now they've made John Garfield a criminal, and since Mr. Garfield is young, resilient, and no end talented, he is making the best of what, after all, is not such a bad situation. In spite of veteran scene-stealers like May Robson and the Dead End Kids (give the boys another year to polish their routines and they can bill themselves as the Six Stooges) it is always Mr. Garfield who carries the show along . . . . It's an elderly plot, all right, but Mr. Garfield is young; he will live it down."

Notes:

They Made Me a Criminal was a remake of a 1933 Warner film, *The Life of Jimmy Dolan,* which featured Douglas Fairbanks, Jr., in the lead, and John Wayne in a bit part. Exterior shooting on *Criminal* began in late summer, 1938, in Palm Desert, California. Director Berkeley said, "It was so hot, we had to stop shooting by noontime, and there were times when the heat was so intense it melted the film in the camera."

They Made Me a Criminal opened at the Strand Theatre in New York on January 20, 1939.

With Gloria Dickson.

With Claude Rains (to left of referee's knee).

With Ann Sheridan, Barbara Pepper.

With Billy Halop.

With Claude Rains, Billy Halop.

3
Blackwell's Island
1939

Credits:

A Warner Bros.-First National Picture. Directed by William McGann. Produced by Hal B. Wallis and Jack L. Warner. Associate producer, Bryan Foy. Screenplay by Crane Wilbur. Based on a story by Crane Wilbur and Lee Katz. Director of photography, Sid Hickox. Film editor, Doug Gould. Dialogue director, Harry Seymour. Assistant director, Elmer Decker. Art director, Stanley Fleischer. Gowns by Howard Shoup. Sound recorder, Leslie G. Hewitt. Musical director, Leo F. Forbstein. Running time, 71 minutes.

Cast:

Tim Haydon	John Garfield
Sunny Walsh	Rosemary Lane
Terry Walsh	Dick Purcell
Thomas McNair	Victor Jory
Bull Bransom	Stanley Fields
Steve Cardigan	Morgan Conway
Warden Stuart Granger	Granville Bates
Brower	Anthony Averill
Pearl Murray	Peggy Shannon
Benny	Charley Foy
Mike Garth	Norman Willis
Rawden	Joe Cunningham
Deputy commissioner	Milburn Stone
Deputy warden Michaels	William Gould
Headkeeper Jameson	Eddy Chandler
Capt. Pederson	Wade Boteler
Hempel	William Davidson
Judge	Walter Young
Ballinger	Leon Ames
Garner	James Spottswood
Mrs. Walsh	Lottie Williams
Cash Sutton	Raymond Bailey
Rico Ide	Jimmy O'Gatty
Nurse	Vera Lewis
Guard	John Hamilton

Synopsis:

Reporter Tim Haydon is on a crusade to rid the New York waterfront of protection racketeer Bull Bransom. After blowing up uncooperative Captain Pederson and his boat, dimwitted Bransom arranges with corrupt official Steve Cardigan to get Tim fired from his job. Tim gets another, however, and attempts to see the hospitalized Pederson. He fails, but meets nurse Sunny Walsh and her policeman brother, Terry. Later Terry is beaten severely by mobsters threatening Pederson's life. Bull is arrested and sent to Blackwell's Island on Terry's and Pederson's evidence.

While Tim and Sunny are falling in love, Cardigan has arranged for Bull to have the run of the prison, which he turns into a resort club for those prisoners who can afford the dues. Bull arranges for the murder of Captain Pederson, and, upon hearing that Terry Walsh is digging up evidence, actually leaves the prison and murders him personally. Tim meets with special prosecutor Ballinger, who is uninterested in pushing an investigation. Tim punches Ballinger and gets himself sentenced to the Island. Forced to pay for simple necessities, poorly fed, the prisoners riot when they see Bull's dogs eating thick steaks. Bull tries to frame Tim as an escapee, but Tim eludes them and leaves the Island in a guard's uniform. He and the new Corrections Commissioner, Thomas McNair, stage a raid on the prison, but Bull escapes. Tim, however, catches up to him and returns him for trial, where Bull is sentenced to ninety-nine years in a real prison.

Review:
Frank S. Nugent in the *New York Times:*
  "The really fictional trimmings are decorative enough: John Garfield as the reporter out to expose the crime ring, Stanley Fields as the moronic public enemy, Granville Bates as the spineless warden and the usual melodramatic windowdressing. It seems almost too Hollywood to be true, but, since most of it is, we New Yorkers will have to grin and admit that the laugh is on us, even though the Warners are pretending they had no one especially in mind."

Notes:
  Blackwell's Island was based on factual occurrences of 1934, when just such a vice and narcotics ring was cleaned out of the New York prison. The newspaper stories Garfield dictates in the film were, for authenticity, written by famed newsman Joseph Jefferson O'Neill.
  Blackwell's Island opened at the Globe Theatre in New York on March 1, 1939.

With Granville Bates, Milburn Stone, Victor Jory, Eddie Chandler, William Gould.

With Stanley Fields.

With Stanley Fields, players.

With Rosemary Lane.

60

4
Juarez
1939

Credits:

A Warner Bros.-First National Picture. Directed by William Dieterle. Produced by Hal B. Wallis. Associate producer, Henry Blanke. Screenplay by John Huston, Aeneas MacKenzie, and Wolfgang Reinhardt. Based in part on the play *Juarez and Maximilian* by Franz Werfel and the book *The Phantom Crown* by Bertita Harding. Director of photography, Tony Gaudio. Music by Erich Wolfgang Korngold. Film editor, Warren Low. Art director, Anton Grot. Costumes by Orry-Kelly. Orchestrations by Leo F. Forbstein. Running time, 125 minutes.

Cast:

Benito Juarez	Paul Muni
Carlotta	Bette Davis
Maximilian Von Hapsburg	Brian Aherne
Napoleon III	Claude Rains
Porfirio Diaz	John Garfield
Empress Eugenie	Gale Sondergaard
Marechal Bazaine	Donald Crisp
Col. Miguel Lopez	Gilbert Roland
Miguel Miramon	Henry O'Neill
Alejandro Uradi	Joseph Calleia
Riva Palacio	Pedro de Cordoba
Jose de Montares	Montagu Love
Dr. Samuel Basch	Harry Davenport
Achille Fould	Walter Fenner
Drouyn de Lhuys	Alexander Leftwich
Countess Battenberg	Georgia Caine
Major Du Pont	Robert Warwick
Senor de Leon	Gennaro Curci
Tomas Mejia	William Wilkerson
Mariano Escobedo	John Miljan
John Bigelow	Hugh Sothern
Carabajal	Irving Pichel
Duc de Morny	Frank Reicher
Marshal Randon	Holmes Herbert
Prince Metternich	Walter Kingsford
Baron von Magnus	Egon Brecher
Lerdo de Tajada	Monte Blue
LeMarc	Louis Calhern
Pepe	Manuel Diaz
Augustin Iturbide	Mickey Kuhn
Camilo	Vladimir Sokoloff
Senor Salas	Fred Malatesta
Tailor	Carlos de Valdez
Coachman	Frank Lackteen
Senator del Valle	Walter O. Stahl
Josefa Iturbide	Lillian Nicholson
Regules	Noble Johnson
Negroni	Martin Garralago
Mr. Harris	Grant Mitchell
Mr. Roberts	Charles Halton

Synopsis:

Maximilian von Hapsburg, Archduke of Austria, having been appointed Emperor of Mexico by Napoleon III, arrives with his wife, Carlotta, in Vera Cruz, where they find the Mexican people violently opposed to the French monarchy. They trust only in the government that their President, Benito Juarez, and his soldiers, including Porfirio Diaz, have been struggling to restore.

Maximilian attempts to remedy the situation by appointing Juarez Secretary of State, a move rejected by both Napoleon and Juarez. Pressured by his government, Maximilian agrees to a law demanding execution for anyone commiting an act of agression against the French monarchy. However, the President of the United States, Abraham Lincoln, supports Juarez, and under the Monroe Doctrine, requests Napoleon to withdraw his forces from Mexico. Napoleon concedes and withdraws his troops, leaving Maximilian to the mercy of the Juaristas.

In an effort to save her husband from impending disaster, Carlotta returns to France to plead with Napoleon to rescue Maximilian. Napoleon refuses to make any attempt to aid the Archduke, and Carlotta, faced with the inevitable loss of her husband, goes insane. Maximilian refuses to leave his now-beloved Mexico, and is captured and executed by the popular forces. Juarez is restored to the Presidency, and pays tribute to Emperor Maximilian, who also loved democracy and Mexico.

Reviews:
Time:

"For Warners' star biographer, Director William Dieterle, 'Juarez' is a bright new feather in an already well-decorated cap."

Franz Hoellering in *The Nation:*

"No one who wants motion pictures which make sense and provide a great experience should miss 'Juarez.' It is the best Hollywood has yet done with a historical theme."

Otis Ferguson in the *New Republic:*

"By Thanksgiving, Warner Brothers' 'Juarez'

should begin to tower as one of the really memorable turkeys. The story of Maximilian in Mexico is a tragic story; but they have made it look like a million dollars' worth of ballroom sets, regimentals, gauze shots, and whiskers."

Newsweek:

"Paul Muni offers a brilliant if necessarily unemotional characterization of the stolid, idealistic Indian. Brian Aherne is splendid as the well-intentioned monarch . . . . Other skillful characterizations are contributed by John Garfield, Claude Rains, Donald Crisp, and Joseph Calleia."

Frank S. Nugent in the *New York Times:*

"Ideologically the new Warner film is faultless . . . . Mr. Dieterle yet must answer the pained charge that he has taken advantage of the remarkable stage presence of the Messrs. Muni, Aherne, Garfield and Rains to mount them, recurrently, on metaphoric soap boxes for purposes of declamation."

Notes:

Juarez was well received, though not so spectacularly as Muni's prior biographical pictures, *The Story of Louis Pasteur* and *The Life of Emile Zola.* Garfield's portrayal was generally acclaimed, although some thought his Bronx accent showed through. The film was listed among the *New York Times'* Ten Best of 1939, and Brian Aherne won a nomination for the Best Supporting Actor Oscar. He lost to Thomas Mitchell for *Stagecoach.*

It might be noted that the role of Porfirio Diaz, which Garfield portrayed, was played by Edward G. Robinson in the 1926 New York production of *Juarez and Maximilian,* upon which *Juarez* was partially based.

Juarez opened at the Hollywood Theatre in New York on April 25, 1939.

With Paul Muni.

With Paul Muni.

With Joseph Calleia, player, Paul Muni.

With extras.

5
Daughters Courageous
1939

Credits:

A Warner Brothers-First National Picture. Directed by Michael Curtiz. Produced by Hal B. Wallis. Associate producer, Henry Blanke. Screenplay by Julius J. and Philip G. Epstein. Suggested by a play by Dorothy Bennett and Irving White. Director of photography, James Wong Howe. Music by Max Steiner. Film editor, Ralph Dawson. Dialogue director, Irving Rapper. Assistant director, Sherry Shourds. Art director, John Hughes. Gowns by Howard Shoup. Makeup by Perc Westmore. Sound recorders, C. A. Riggs and Oliver S. Garretson. Orchestrations by Ray Heindorf. Musical director, Leo F. Forbstein. Running time, 107 minutes.

Cast:

Gabriel Lopez	John Garfield
Jim Masters	Claude Rains
Buff Masters	Priscilla Lane
Tinka Masters	Rosemary Lane
Linda Masters	Lola Lane
Cora Masters	Gale Page
Johnny Heming	Jeffrey Lynn
Nan Masters	Fay Bainter
Sam Sloane	Donald Crisp
Penny	May Robson
George	Frank McHugh
Eddie Moore	Dick Foran
Manuel Lopez	George Humbert
Judge Hornsby	Berton Churchill

Synopsis:

Nan Masters has raised her four daughters, Buff, Tinka, Linda, and Cora, alone since her husband, Jim, abandoned them twenty years earlier. Nan accepts the marriage proposal of well-to-do businessman Sam Sloane, and her daughters give their approval. Nan and Buff go to court to aid their fisherman friend Manuel Lopez, whose son Gabriel has been arrested for peddling fraudulent teeth from Moby Dick. When told that Moby Dick was the fictional creation of an author, wiseguy Gabe replies that "he made him seem very real to me." Gabe is released and, walking Buff home, thinks nothing of asking her to buy him a beer, which she does. Intrigued by Gabe's nonconformity, Buff asks him to take her out. He answers noncommittally.

That evening, the family sits down to dinner with their guest, Sam, when Jim Masters returns without warning. Ignored by his daughters, Jim is allowed to stay for a few days. He is left alone when everyone goes out on the town, including Buff, who has given up waiting for Gabe and goes out with suitor Johnny Heming. Gabe shows up later and becomes friendly with Jim, then goes into town to find Buff. When he locates her, she leaves Johnny for Gabe, who invites her to spend the next day with him on his boat.

65

On the following day, Buff, against her mother's wishes, goes with Gabe, while Jim uses his charm to crumble his daughters' antagonism toward him. He also lies to cover Buff's date with Gabe. Buff returns and, losing her resistance also, tells Jim she loves Gabe. Later, Sam takes Jim aside and, referring to Jim's constant urge to wander, asks him to leave now, for everyone's sake.

Nan demands that Buff drop Gabe, but she refuses and the two decide to elope. Jim gives them his blessing and, later, tells Nan he wants to stay. She tells him of the opportunities Sam offers the girls, and of her fears that Gabe will someday give in to his wanderlust and desert Buff. Jim recognizes the truth and decides to leave, asking Gabe to goe with him. Buff waits for Gabe, but Johnny tells her he is gone and that she should marry Johnny instead. They go together to the wedding of Nan and Sam and, as the vows are said, Gabe and Jim sell Moby Dick's tooth for their passage out of town.

Reviews:
Philip Hartung in *Commonweal:*

"John Garfield does an extremely good job with his role. It's too bad that motivations throughout weren't considered more carefully; this cast is worthy of something better than all this shallowness."

Newsweek:

The film's effect is spirited and youthful, with a good cast making the most of the story's emotions. In any case, 'Daughters Courageous' is successful enough to justify the Warners in planning at least two sequels — one with the four girls as wives, the other as mothers. Tempus fugit."

Frank S. Nugent in the *New York Times:*

"Perhaps the conjuration of mood is more deliberate here than it had been in 'Four Daughters.' In Mr. Garfield's case, at least, the role's concept shrieks of attempted duplication. . . . It is a thoroughly pleasant entertainment — howbeit reminiscent — with a thoroughly pleasant cast to grace it. Mr. Rains is the best part of it, but Fay Bainter as the mother, Priscilla Lane as the liveliest of the daughters, Mr. Garfield as the intruder, Donald Crisp as the solid citizen, and the others are scarcely less deserving."

Notes:

One of the working titles for *Daughters Courageous* was *Family Reunion,* which aptly described this regathering of the cast (but not the characters) of *Four Daughters.*

Daughters Courageous opened at the Strand Theatre in New York on June 23, 1939.

With Claude Rains, Priscilla Lane, Fay Bainter, Lola Lane, Gale Page, Donald Crisp, Dick Foran, Frank McHugh, Rosemary Lane.

Daughters Courageous

JOHN GARFIELD CLAUDE RAINS·JEFFREY LYNN·FAY BAINTER·DONALD CRISP·MAY ROBSON
and THE "FOUR DAUGHTERS"
PRISCILLA LANE · ROSEMARY LANE · LOLA LANE
GALE PAGE Directed by MICHAEL CURTIZ PRESENTED BY **WARNER BROS.**

With Priscilla Lane.

With Priscilla Lane.

6
Dust Be My Destiny

1939

Credits:

A Warner Bros.-First National Picture. Directed by Lewis Seiler. Produced by Louis F. Edelman. Screenplay by Robert Rossen. Based on the novel by Jerome Odlum. Director of photography, James Wong Howe. Music by Max Steiner. Film editor, Warren Low. Dialogue director, Irving Rapper. Assistant director, William Kissel. Art director, Hugh Reticker. Costumes by Milo Anderson. Make-up by Perc Westmore. Special effects by Byron Haskin. Sound recorder, Robert B. Lee. Orchestrations by Hugo Friedhofer. Musical director, Leo F. Forbstein. Running time, 88 minutes.

Cast:

Joe Bell	John Garfield
Mabel	Priscilla Lane
Mike Leonard	Alan Hale
Caruthers	Frank McHugh
Hank	Billy Halop
Jimmy	Bobby Jordan
Pop	Charlie Grapewin
Nick	Henry Armetta
Charlie	Stanley Ridges
Prosecutor	John Litel
Warden	John Hamilton
Thug	Ward Bond
Defense attorney	Moroni Olsen
Doc Saunders	Victor Killian
Abe Connors	Frank Jaquet
Shopkeeper	Ferike Boros
Venetti	Marc Lawrence
Magistrate	Arthur Aylesworth
Warden	William Davidson
Judge	George Irving
Pawnshop owner	Charles Halton

Synopsis:

Joe Bell and two other drifters, Hank and Jimmy, are caught hopping a ride on a freight train. Joe is apprehended and sent to a prison work farm. While there, he meets Mabel, the step-daughter of the cruel prison foreman, Charlie. Charlie is an alcoholic with a weak heart. Joe and Mabel fall in love, but one day Charlie catches them together and Joe is forced to fight him. Charlie's weak heart gives out and he dies. Fearing that he will be charged with murder, Joe escapes with Mabel.

The two of them travel around, seeking work and struggling to survive. Joe cannot get a job, and he is near total despair when they receive an offer of a houseful of free furniture if they will agree to marry on stage at a local theatre. The consent and are married amid popping flashbulbs and jeering crowds. But Joe is offered a job by a new friend, Mike Leonard, and with the money and furniture, life begins to look good to the pair.

Before Joe and Mabel can get used to their good fortune, a newspaper prints a picture of their wedding, and the police catch up with Joe. He is brought to trial, but by the efforts of the defense attorney and the testimony of his new friends, he is acquitted. He and Mabel leave the court to start a fresh life.

Reviews:

Philip T. Hartung in *Commonweal:*

"John Garfield and Priscilla Lane give such appealing performances in 'Dust Be My Destiny' that they almost make this melodrama convincing. Things go from very bad to much worse as the cards are obviously stacked against embittered Joe. You can't believe the false story any more than can the sneering audience in the film believe in the wedding that unites Joe and Mabel on the stage of a cheap theatre."

Frank S. Nugent in the *New York Times:*

"John Garfield, official gall-and-wormwood taster for the Warners, is sipping another bitter brew at the Strand in 'Dust Be My Destiny.' Personally, we're tired of the formula . . . . Mr. Garfield, Miss Lane, Stanley Ridges as the prison foreman, Henry Armetta as proprietor of a diner, Alan Hale as a city editor, and most of the others have played it well enough, although we detect signs in Mr. Garfield of taking even his cynicism cynically, and of weariness in Miss Lane at having to redeem Mr. Garfield all over again."

Notes:

Although not very original in theme, *Dust Be My Destiny* seems to be the Garfield film most remembered by today's public. It had an excellent, if typical, Warner cast, including John Hamilton, later to play Perry White in the "Superman" TV series, in one of the few instances in which Warners did *not* cast him as a judge.

Dust Be My Destiny opened at the Strand Theatre, in New York on October 6, 1939.

With Players.

With Priscilla Lane, player.

With Priscilla Lane, Henry Armetta.

With Henry Armetta, Priscilla Lane.

With Henry Armetta, Priscilla Lane, Alan Hale.

7
Four Wives
1939

Credits:

A Warner Bros.-First National Picture. Directed by Michael Curtiz. Produced by Hal B. Wallis. Associate producer, Henry Blanke. Screenplay by Julius J. and Philip G. Epstein and Maurice Hanline. Based on the book *Sister Act* by Fannie Hurst. Director of photography, Sol Polito. Music by Max Steiner. Film editor, Ralph Dawson. Dialogue director, Jo Graham. Assistant director, Sherry Shourds. Art director, John Hughes. Costumes by Howard Shoup. Make-up by Perc Westmore. Sound recorder, Oliver S. Garretson. Orchestrations by Hugo Friedhofer and Ray Heindorf. Musical director, Leo F. Forbstein. "Mickey Borden's Theme" by Max Rabinowitsh. Running time, 110 minutes.

Cast:

Adam Lemp	Claude Rains
Ann Lemp	Priscilla Lane
Kay Lemp	Rosemary Lane
Thea Lemp Crowley	Lola Lane
Emma Lemp Talbot	Gale Page
Felix Deitz	Jeffrey Lynn
Dr. Clinton Forrest, Jr.	Eddie Albert
Aunt Etta	May Robson
Ben Crowley	Frank McHugh
Ernest Talbot	Dick Foran
Dr. Clinton Forrest, Sr.	Henry O'Neill
Mrs. Ridgefield	Vera Lewis
Frank	John Qualen
Mathilde	Ruth Tobey
Joe	Olin Howland
Laboratory man	George Reeves
Mickey Borden	John Garfield

Synopsis:

Adam Lemp and his daughters have gone on with life after Mickey Borden's death. Thea has married Ben Crowley and Emma has married Ernest Talbot. Kay has a new beau, Dr. Clinton Forrest, Jr., and after a time, Mickey Borden's widow, Ann, has fallen in love with and become engaged to composer Felix Deitz. Felix has completed the unfinished symphony Mickey left behind. The situation is complicated, however, when on the day of the couple's engagement, Ann discovers that she is pregnant with Mickey's child.

At first unsure of what to do, Ann soon realizes the fact that Mickey wanted only her happiness. She marries Felix and Kay marries her doctor, Clinton.

Reviews:

Philip T. Hartung in *Commonweal:*

Four Wives does not have the charming vignette quality of the first film or anything that compares with the startling entrance and performance of John Garfield as Mickey Borden, the cynical musical genius who eloped with Ann (Priscilla Lane), but it does have an interesting solution and the same friendly, warm family theme."

Time:

"This time maternal instinct defeats the considerable ingenuity with which, in *Four Daughters,* Director Michael Curtiz managed to keep cinemaudiences straight about, and interested in, the doings of four leading characters in one picture."

Frank S. Nugent in the *New York Times:*

"Sequels so rarely even approximate the quality of their originals that the Warners deserve a special word of commendation this morning for their 'Four Wives,' the Strand's inevitable aftermath to the 'Four Daughters' which appeared on most of the ten-best lists last year. For it is a singularly happy film, well-written, well-directed, and well-played .... John Garfield appears briefly as the ghost of his former proud self."

Notes:

Garfield was officially unbilled in *Four Wives,* appearing only in flashback or in photographs. He did not appear in the sequels to come.

Four Wives opened at the Strand Theatre in New York on December 22, 1939.

Garfield is in the framed photograph. With May Robson, Rosemary Lane, Lola Lane, Gale Page, Claude Rains.

8
Castle on the Hudson
1940

Credits:

A Warner Bros. Picture. Directed by Anatole Litvak. Produced by Hal B. Wallis. Associate producer, Samuel Bischoff. Screenplay by Seton I. Miller, Brown Holmes, and Cortney Terrett. Based on the book *20,000 Years in Sing Sing,* by Warden Lewis E. Lawes. Director of photography, Arthur Edeson. Music by Adolph Deutsch. Film editor, Thomas Richards. Dialogue director, Irving Rapper. Assistant director, Chuck Hansen. Art director, John Hughes. Costumes by Howard Shoup. Makeup by Perc Westmore. Special effects by Byron Haskin. Sound recorder, Robert B. Lee. Orchestrations by Ray Heindorf. Musical director, Leo F. Forbstein. Running time, 77 minutes.

Cast:

Tommy Gordon	John Garfield
Kay	Ann Sheridan
Warden Long	Pat O'Brien
Steven Rockford	Burgess Meredith
District Attorney	Henry O'Neill
Ed Crowley	Jerome Cowan
Mike Cagle	Guinn "Big Boy" Williams
Chaplain	John Litel
Ann Rockford	Margot Stevenson
Ragan	Willard Robertson
Black Jack	Edward Pawley
Pete	Billy Wayne
Mrs. Long	Nedda Harrington
Principal keeper	Wade Boteler
Goldie	Barbara Pepper
Joe Morris	Robert Strange
Clerk	John Ridgely
Clerk	Frank Faylen
Guard	James Flavin
Detective	Robert Homans
Detective	Emmett Vogan

Synopsis:

Mobster Tommy Gordon is not worried about being sentenced to Sing Sing because he believes his political pals will get him a fast parole. He tells his girlfriend, Kay, not to worry. He makes no effort to reform in prison, and after causing a near-riot is given three months in solitary confinement by Warden Long, a dedicated prison reformer. After the ninety days in solitary, Tommy concedes that his friends have deserted him, and he joins a group of convicts planning to escape. He changes his mind, however, when he learns that the break is planned for a day he considers unlucky. A stool-pigeon reveals the escape-plan to the warden, and all the convicts are killed or captured.

Meanwhile, Kay is seriously injured in a car crash, and Warden Long allows Tommy to visit her unguarded. Tommy promises to return that night.

Two detectives, unaware of his pass, see Tommy and follow him. While visiting Kay, Tommy encounters Ed Crowley, the man responsible for sending him to prison and leaving him there. A fight ensues and Kay shoots Crowley. Tommy escapes, and the detectives rush in on time to hear Crowley accuse Tommy of the shooting. Crowley dies, and Kay cannot convince anyone of the truth.

Tommy does not return to prison, and Warden Long faces dismissal for releasing him. Hearing of this, Tommy returns and confesses the killing of Crowley in order to protect Kay. He is convicted and sentenced to die in the electric chair.

Review:

B. R. Crisler in the *New York Times:*

"This is merely a routine notice that Mr. John Garfield, formerly of the Group Theatre, who was recently sentenced to a term in Warner Brothers pictures, is still in prison. . . . The literary source is still that supreme cinematic quarry of quarries, '20,000 Years in Sing Sing.' They don't even bother to change the furniture in the Warden's office; they only change the Warden, who, this time, is Pat O'Brien — and a fine broth of a Warden he is, too; a regular fellow, though he is on the side of the law. Mr. Garfield, who seems to be wearing a trifle thin, for some reason — can it be possible that he has been a little over-built as a screen personality? — is the tough but golden-hearted prisoner who goes to the deathhouse trailing wisecracks like cigarette ashes . . . . You have met them all before, and whether you care to renew the acquaintance or not, here is an excellent opportunity."

Notes:

Castle on the Hudson is a remake of Warners' 1933 *20,000 Years in Sing Sing*, which featured Spencer Tracy, Bette Davis, and Arthur Byron in the Garfield-Sheridan-O'Brien roles. It also bears a strong resemblance to 1934's *Manhattan Melodrama. Castle,* though trite in theme, featured fine performances, especially by Burgess Meredith and Guinn Williams as the harmonica-playing prisoner on Death Row.

Castle on the Hudson opened at the Globe Theatre in New York on March 3, 1940.

With Jerome Cowan.

With Robert Homans, Emmett Vogan.

With Burgess Meredith.

With Pat O' Brien, Ann Sheridan.

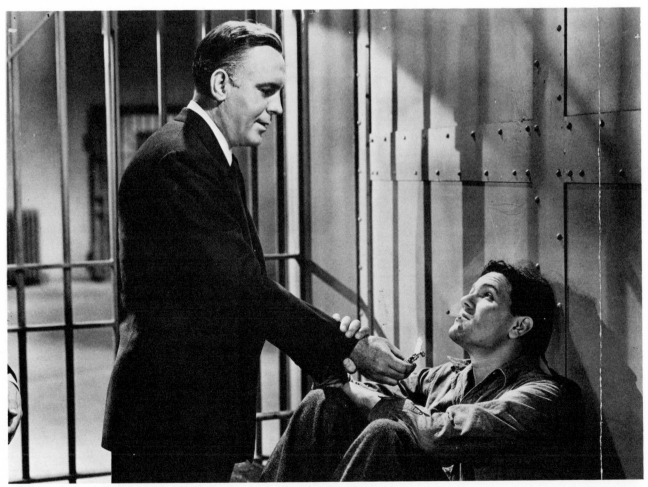

With Pat O' Brien.

9
Saturday's Children
1940

Credits:

A Warner Bros. Picture. Directed by Vincent Sherman. Produced by Jack L. Warner and Hal B. Wallis. Associate producer, Henry Blanke. Screenplay by Julius J. Epstein and Philip G. Epstein. Based on the play by Maxwell Anderson. Director of photography, James Wong Howe. Film editor, Owen Marks. Running time, 101 minutes.

Cast:

Rims O'Neill	John Garfield
Bobby Halevy	Anne Shirley
Mr. Halevy	Claude Rains
Florrie Sands	Lee Patrick
Herbie Smith	George Tobias
Willie Sands	Roscoe Karns
Gertrude Mills	Dennie Moore
Mrs. Halevy	Elizabeth Risdon
Mr. Norman	Berton Churchill
1st carpenter	John Qualen
2nd carpenter	Tom Dugan
Mr. MacReady	John Ridgely
Mrs. MacReady	Margot Stevenson
Boy	Claude Wisberg
Mac	Jack Mower
Elevator operator	Glen Cavender
Joe	Gus Glassmire
Cabby	Frank Faylen
Girl	Nell O'Day
Mailman	Creighton Hale
Nurse	Maris Wrixon
Nurse	Lucille Fairbanks
Nightwatchman	Paul Panzer
Doctor	Sam Flint

Synopsis:

The eccentric Halevy family lives in a railroad flat on the wrong side of Manhattan's subway tracks. Pretty Bobby Halevy loves Rims O'Neill, a shy, half-educated, half-awake fellow who invents gadgets that never work and dreams of going to Manila to try to turn hemp into silk. Mr. Halevy, a bookkeeper, has spent a lifetime working dully in a mail-order house. Mrs. Halevy, a movie-nut, has spent a lifetime knitting her husband a sweater, but has never finished it. Also among the clan is cheap, dissatisfied Florrie Halevy Sands, who henpecks her bill-collector husband Willie.

Florrie talks Bobby into tricking Rims into marrying her just before he is starting for Manila. The two marry, and Rims and Bobby live happily for a time in a $22.50 flat over a garage. Then Bobby loses her job, Rims takes a cut, the bills pile up, and the quarrels begin. When things reach a peak of disorder, Rims leaves Bobby. He reaches the depths of despair and attempts to commit suicide, but Mr. Halevy stops him and informs him that Bobby is going to have a baby. Rims returns to Bobby and the two resolve to start over and try harder.

Reviews:

Philip T. Hartung in *Commonweal:*

"Bachelors will be suspicious of their next few dates after they see the tactics Anne Shirley uses in 'Saturday's Children' to rope in John Garfield. However, Anne probably gets what she deserves when her marriage flounders. Director Vincent Sherman and Scriptwriters Julius and Philip Epstein have made an interesting movie out of Maxwell Anderson's play; although the tacked-on attempted suicide ending almost spoils the realistic, humorous, pathetic picture of a Mr. and Mrs. Average Man who, being Saturday's Children, are full of woe. The film teaches that marriage is more than a love affair and honeymoon. Anne Shirley turns in a fine performance as the girl who lies to get her man and then has difficulty holding him. John Garfield shows that he can play with feeling other roles than the convict or snotty chip-on-the-shoulder types he has been portraying."

Bosley Crowther in the *New York Times:*

"Particular praise is in store for John Garfield, the sallow Romeo with the sad face and troubled soul, who falls into the part of the harassed young lover as though it had been written for him alone, and to Anne Shirley, who endows the little wife with heroic integrity and strength of character. It is a rich and flavorsome picture of New York's subway society, this 'Saturday's Children,' marred only by one of those contrived, self-sacrificial endings. But in gratitude for the rest of it, we'll just pass over that."

Notes:

Maxwell Anderson's play had been filmed twice before, in 1929, and in 1935 under the title *Maybe It's Love.*

Saturday's Children opened at the Strand Theatre in New York on May 4, 1940.

With Anne Shirley, players.

With Claude Rains, Anne Shirley.

With Ann Shirley, Tom Dugan, John Qualen.

With Anne Shirley.

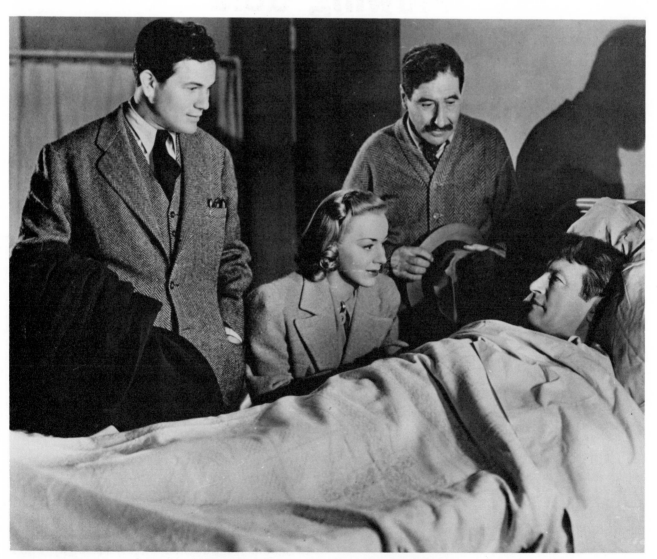

With Anne Shirley, Gus Glassmire, Claude Rains.

10
Flowing Gold
1940

Credits:

A Warner Bros. Picture. Directed by Alfred E. Green. Produced by Bryan Foy. Associate producer, William Jacobs. Screenplay by Kenneth Gamet. Based on the novel by Rex Beach. Director of photography, Sid Hickox. Music by Adolph Deutsch. Film editor, James Gibbon. Dialogue director, Hugh MacMullan. Assistant director, Jesse Hibbs. Art director, Hugh Reticker. Special effects by Byron Haskin and Willard Van Enger. Orchestrations by Leo F. Forbstein. Running time, 82 minutes.

Cast:

Johnny Blake	John Garfield
Linda Chalmers	Frances Farmer
Hap O'Conner	Pat O'Brien
Wildcat Chalmers	Raymond Walburn
Hot Rocks	Cliff Edwards
Petunia	Tom Kennedy
Charles Hammond	Granville Bates
Tillie	Jody Gilbert
Collins	Edward Pawley
Mike Brannigan	Frank Mayo
Joe	William Marshall
Luke	Sol Gorss
Nurse	Virginia Sale
Sheriff	John Alexander

Synopsis:

Johnny Blake is dodging the law for a trumped-up murder charge. His flight lands him in the oilfields, where he gets a job with gruff, but kind-hearted Hap O'Connor. O'Connor is a straw boss in charge of a gang of roughnecks who shuttle from field to field drilling wells. Johnny and Hap become close friends after Johnny saves Hap's life during a well accident. Hap's girlfriend, Linda, develops a strong dislike for Johnny because of his smart-aleck attitude and because he derisively calls her "freckle-nose." But before much time can pass, she realizes that she really loves Johnny. Hap turns on Johnny for pilfering his girl. Johnny regains Hap's respect by his bravery in fighting an oil-well fire. Hap realizes that Johnny will make Linda happier, and he gives the couple his blessing while putting the police on the wrong track.

Reviews:

Philip T. Hartung in *Commonweal:*

'Flowing Gold' . . . is just typical action cinema. . . . Pat O'Brien comes very close again to giving a good performance without trying very hard one way or the other. John Garfield, after his last winter's ill-fated fling on Broadway, is back doing extremely well with the same old role: the chip-on-the-shoulder, hard-fisted, sweaty-faced guy who is still fleeing from the police because of some crime he committed a couple of years back."

Theodore Strauss in the *New York Times:*

"There is a moment toward the end of 'Flowing Gold,' now at the Globe, when John Garfield looks up dourly at the salt-water spouting from a newly-opened well and remarks: "We hit the jackpot, and there wasn't any nickels." Let that serve as a simile for this shakily written and shakily directed film . . . . Warners have drilled for a gusher and brought up a trickle . . . . In this trite tale, Mr. O'Brien is still his accustomed hard-boiled self, Miss Farmer is still a very striking lady who is also a good actress when relaxed, and Mr. Garfield is still Mr. Garfield, which is good enough to make one wish that his producers would cease casting him in the same role, film after film. In fact, we don't think Mr. Garfield was running away from a murder rap at all. He was just a fugitive from Warners'.'

Notes:

Flowing Gold was filmed once before, in 1924. Frances Farmer was another ex-member of the Group Theatre. This was one of her few films before her harrowing experiences with mental illness, recounted in her autobiography, *Will There Really Be A Morning?*

Flowing Gold opened at the Globe Theatre in New York on September 1, 1940.

With Frances Farmer, Pat O' Brien.

With Frances Farmer.

With Frances Farmer, Pat O' Brien.

With Pat O' Brien, player.

11
East of the River

1940

Credits:

A Warner Bros.-First National Picture. Directed by Alfred E. Green. Produced by Bryan Foy. Associate producer, Harland Thompson. Screenplay by Fred Niblo, Jr. Based on a story by John Fante and Ross B. Wills. Director of photography, Sid Hickox. Music by Adolph Deutsch. Film editor, Thomas Pratt. Dialogue director, Hugh MacMullan. Assistant director, Les Guthrie. Art director, Hugh Reticker. Gowns by Howard Shoup. Makeup by Perc Westmore. Sound recorder, Stanley Jones. Musical director, Leo F. Forbstein. Technical advisor, Marie Jenardi. Running time, 73 minutes.

Cast:

Joe Lorenzo	John Garfield
Laurie Romayne	Brenda Marshall
Teresa Lorenzo	Marjorie Rambeau
Tony	George Tobias
Nick Lorenzo	William Lundigan
Judge Davis	Moroni Olsen
Cy Turner	Douglas Fowley
Scarfi	Jack LaRue
"No Neck" Griswold	Jack Carr
Balmy	Paul Guilfoyle
Warden	Russell Hicks
Customer	Charles Foy
Henchman	Ralph Volkie
Henchman	Jimmy O'Gatty
Patrolman Shanahan	Robert Homans
Joe (as a boy)	Joe Conti
Nick (as a boy)	O'Neill Nolan
Guide	Frank Faylen
Usher	William Marshall
Dink Rogers	Murray Alper
Cop	Roy Barcroft
Railroad guard	Eddy Chandler

Synopsis:

In 1927, young Joe Lorenzo and his pal Nick are arrested for hopping a freight and assaulting a guard. The pleas of Joe's mother gain him another chance, and Mrs. Lorenzo adopts the homeless Nick in order to save him from reform school. Years later, Nick has grown into a college honor student, while Joe is doing time in California. Joe is released from prison in time to attend Nick's graduation in New York. Bitter about the two crooks who framed him, Cy and Scarfi, Joe returns home with his girl, Laurie, vowing vengeance. Joe soon encounters Cy and Scarfi, who propose that he join them on a robbery. Joe agrees, but then sets them up for the police. Though the gangsters plan to doublecross Joe, their own plans are fouled and Scarfi is caught. Cy escapes and Joe plans to leave for California. Laurie, however, has changed her ways and decides to stay with Mama. Joe leaves for the West. Some time later, Nick and Laurie begin to date and then to fall in love. In Tijuana, Joe receives Laurie's letter informing him of the upcoming marriage. He returns in anger and demands that Laurie go with him, threatening to reveal her past to Nick. She gives in to protect Nick, and the next day she and Joe tell Nick that the wedding is off.

When Mama learns of this, she slaps Joe and tells him he is a disgrace to her. Joe turns about, but when he goes to tell Laurie the good news, he finds her being grilled by Cy's gang. He tells her that she can marry Nick, and asks Cy to be allowed to take her to the wedding. The whole gang accompanies them to the church, where Joe says goodbye to Mama and then, suddenly, punches a passing policeman. This draws many more police, who arrest Joe as the gang rushes off and the wedding proceeds.

REVIEWS:

Leonard Maltin in *TV Movies*

"Another variation of *Manhattan Melodrama,* with two childhood pals growing up on opposite sides of the law. Rambeau gives a fine performance."

Theodore Strauss in the *New York Times:*

"The war of attrition between John Garfield and the law of the realm — or is it just the Warner Brothers? — seems perilously close to its final stages in 'East of the River,' now at the Globe . . . . It is this corner's business to describe their latest collaboration as a contrived and hackneyed repetition of Mr. Garfield's previous case histories of wastrels, each with a streak of nobility which the scenarists reveal by releasing a sliding panel in the plot . . . . Mr. Garfield can still make a line like "When you're in the swamps, you look out for snakes" sound like authentic Second Avenue philosophy . . . . Isn't it time that the Warners allowed Mr. Garfield really to reform — and stay that way?"

Notes:

East of the River was originally titled *Mama Raviola* and scheduled for James Cagney, who turned it down.

East of the River opened at the Globe Theatre in New York on October 27, 1940.

With players.

With Douglas Fowley, Jack La Rue.

With William Lundigan, Marjorie Rambeau, Brenda Marshall.

With Douglas Fowley, Brenda Marshall.

12
The Sea Wolf

1941

Credits:

A Warner Bros.-First National Picture. Directed by Michael Curtiz. Produced by Jack L. Warner and Hal B. Wallis. Associate producer, Henry Blanke. Screenplay by Robert Rossen. Based on the novel by Jack London. Director of photography, Sol Polito. Music by Erich Wolfgang Korngold. Film editor, George Amy. Art director, Anton Grot. Special effects by Byron Haskin and H. F. Koenekamp. Running time, 100 minutes.

Cast:

Wolf Larsen	Edward G. Robinson
George Leach	John Garfield
Ruth Webster	Ida Lupino
Humphrey van Weyden	Alexander Knox
Dr. Louie Prescott	Gene Lockhart
Cooky	Barry Fitzgerald
Johnson	Stanley Ridges
Svenson	Francis McDonald
Harrison	Howard da Silva
Smoke	Frank Lackteen
Young sailor	David Bruce
Helmsman	Wilfred Lucas
Sailor	Louis Mason
Agent	Ralf Harolde
Crewman	Dutch Hendrian
1st detective	Cliff Clark
2nd detective	William Gould
First mate	Charles Sullivan
Pickpocket	Ernie Adams
Singer	Jeane Cowan
Crewman	Ethan Laidlaw

Synopsis:

Writer Humphrey van Weyden and fugitive Ruth Webster are rescued from a ferry sinking in San Francisco Bay by the sealer *Ghost,* a mysterious ship commanded by a cruel captain named Wolf Larsen. Larsen passes time by tormenting George Leach, the cabin boy, who has signed aboard the *Ghost* to escape the police. The crew mutinies under Wolf's bestial treatment, attempting unsuccessfully to kill Larsen. The mutiny fails, and Ruth, George, and van Weyden escape the ship in a small boat, only to find that Larsen has destroyed their provisions. After many days, they find they have drifted back to the *Ghost,* slowly sinking after an attack by Wolf's brother and enemy. In search of food and water, George boards the empty ship, but fails to return. Ruth and van Weyden look for him, finding him locked in the galley, where the rising water will soon drown him. Van Weyden finds Larsen alone in his cabin, slowly going blind. Van Weyden promises to stay with Larsen as the ship goes down in exchange for the key, which he slips through the door to Ruth. She frees George and they row away to a nearby island as the *Ghost* goes down.

Reviews:

Philip T. Hartung in *Commonweal:*

"The *Ghost* is manned by the hardest bunch of derelicts, convicts, thugs as ever sailed the seas . . . . To lead the revolt against the tyrannical captain's cruelty, there is tough, weather-beaten John Garfield who gives and takes in another of those swell performances that really is the continuation of the same embittered, fleeing-from-the-police, down-on-everyone role."

Otis Ferguson in *The New Republic:*

"Here in the new version the story is given a $900,000 production. It has the characters of Edward G. Robinson, Ida Lupino, Barry Fitzgerald, Gene Lockhart, John Garfield, Alexander Knox, and Stanley Ridges. All are good, the first four particularly . . . . Everything is there. But where is the original wonder?"

Newsweek:

"The current version is — if anything — more brutal than the old silent film, but only rarely credible; aside from a fine cast, its principal contribution to entertainment is a scriptful of violence for excitement's sake."

Time:

"For restless cinemaddicts whom only blood and thunder can quiet, *The Sea Wolf* should prove a strong sedative."

Bosley Crowther in the *New York Times:*

" . . . . we don't recall that he [Wolf Larsen] has ever been presented with such scrupulous psychological respect as he is in the Warners' current version of 'The Sea Wolf.' . . . It draws a forbidding picture of oppressive life at sea . . . Some of it is too heavily drenched with theatrical villainy, and Mr. Robinson occasionally overacts his part. But, on the whole, the slapping and cuffing are done with impressive virility and in a manner distinctive to Warner films. John Garfield plays the part of a recalcitrant crewman with concentrated spite."

Notes:

Jack London's classic novel has been filmed seven times, more or less. True, the sixth version, *Barricade* (1950), took place in the Sierra mountains, but the storyline was essentially the same. First filmed in 1913, there were other versions in 1920, 1925, 1930, and 1958, with another in production for 1977. A press preview of the 1941 version was held at sea, between Los Angeles and San Francisco, with Garfield, Robinson, and Lupino attending. The special guest was Hobart Bosworth, who played Wolf Larsen in the 1913 production. This was the only film in which Garfield worked with Edward G. Robinson.

The Sea Wolf opened at the Strand Theatre in New York on March 21, 1941.

With Barry Fitzgerald, Edward G. Robinson, Gene Lockhart, Ida Lupino, Alexander Knox.

With Ida Lupino, Edward G. Robinson.

With Edward G. Robinson, Louis Mason, Dutch Hendrian.

With Dutch Hendrian, Ida Lupino, Howard da Silva, crewmen.

With Edward G. Robinson, Ida Lupino.

13
Out of the Fog
1941

Credits:

A Warner Bros. Picture. Directed by Anatole Litvak. Produced by Hal B. Wallis. Associate producer, Henry Blanke. Screenplay by Robert Rossen, Jerry Wald, and Richard Macauley. Based on the play *The Gentle People,* by Irwin Shaw. Director of photography, James Wong Howe. Film editor, Warren Low. Dialogue director, Jo Graham. Assistant director, Lee Katz. Art director, Carl Jules Weyl. Special effects by Rex Wimpy. Orchestrations by Leo F. Forbstein. Running time, 93 minutes.

Cast:

Stella Goodwin	Ida Lupino
Harold Goff	John Garfield
Jonah Goodwin	Thomas Mitchell
George Watkins	Eddie Albert
Olaf Knudsen	John Qualen
Igor Propotkin	George Tobias
Florence Goodwin	Aline MacMahon
Officer Magruder	Robert Homans
Sam Pepper	Bernard Gorcey
Eddie	Leo Gorcey
Boss	Ben Welden
Judge	Paul Harvey
District attorney	Jerome Cowan
Caroline Pomponette	Odette Myrtil
Clerk	Murray Alper
Reporter	Charles Drake
Detective	Charles Wilson
Detective	Jack Mower
Bublitchki	Konstantin Sankar
Kibitzer	James Conlin
Dancer	Mayta Palmera
Morgue attendant	Herbert Heywood

Synopsis:

Jonah Goodwin and Olaf Knudsen are simple fishermen in Long Island's Sheepshead Bay. They are trying to succeed with their own business, for which they have only recently purchased a new boat. As things begin to look up, they are suddenly confronted by gangster Harold Goff, who forces them to buy "boat protection," or risk losing their new vessel. Goff is cruel and pitiless toward the two men, but he shows some slight signs of humanity in falling in love with Goodwin's daughter Stella. Stella returns his affection, unaware of his treatment of her father. Jonah and Olaf are afraid to go to the authorities about Goff's extortion, for fear that he will get off lightly and then revenge himself. After much discussion, they decide to take the law into their own hands and kill Goff themselves. They convince him to accompany them in their boat out onto the bay. As they prepare to murder Goff, he slips and accidentally falls overboard and drowns in the dark waters of the bay. Their consciences still clean, Jonah and Olaf sail back to the wharf to continue their business venture.

Reviews:
John Mosher in the *New Yorker:*

"John Garfield, as the racketeer, doesn't quite suggest, as Franchot Tone did [in the play], that he spends his loot at the Stork Club or El Morocco. One suspects simpler haunts, and even noisier ones, would be his choice, which in no way detracts from the reality of the piece .... This is one case where a good play makes for a good movie, which is by no means a usual rule."

Newsweek:

"While the Warner Brothers' *Out of the Fog* is not the showman's answer to the current box-office slump, it is one of the worthiest films to come out of Hollywood for several undistinguished months .... The theme is refreshingly different from the tired tried-and-true formulas."
Philip T. Hartung in *Commonweal:*

"This drama of Long Island's Sheepshead Bay has excellent sets and a group of fine cinema actors who work well under Anatole Litvak's direction. But in spite of a good production, this picture lacks conviction."

Bosley Crowther in the *New York Times:*

"'Out of the Fog' is a heavy and dreary recital of largely synthetic woes, laced with moderate suspense and spotted here and there with humor. It doesn't even come close to being a really good film, and, if you want the honest truth, it is literally as old-fashioned as sin .... It has moments of sinister impact, especially when John Garfield as the gangster is turning on the heat. Mr. Garfield is a sleek and vicious character, a most convincing small-time racketeer .... Thomas Mitchell plays the father in a droopily sentimental vein, and John Qualen is his meek and fearful side-kick in a way that only John Qualen can be."

Notes:

In the original Shaw play, the racketeer is murdered by the two fishermen, a plot line changed for the film censors, who could not allow *anyone* to get away with premeditated murder, no matter who the victim was.

Out of the Fog opened at the Strand Theatre in New York on June 20, 1941.

With Leo Gorcey.

With Eddie Albert, Ida Lupino.

With Ida Lupino.

14
Dangerously They Live
1942

Credits:

A Warner Bros. Picture. Directed by Robert Florey. Produced by Bryan Foy. Associate producer, Ben Stoloff. Screenplay by Marion Parsonnet. Based on the novel *Remember Tomorrow* by Marion Parsonnet. Director of Photography, L. William O'Connell. Film editor, Les Guthrie. Art director, Hugh Reticker. Running time, 71 minutes.

Cast:

Dr. Michael Lewis	John Garfield
Jane	Nancy Coleman
Dr. Ingersoll	Raymond Massey
Mr. Goodwin	Moroni Olsen
Nurse Johnson	Lee Patrick
Steiner	Christian Rub
Mrs. Steiner	Ilka Gruning
Dr. Murdock	Roland Drew
Jarvis	Frank Reicher
Dawson	Esther Dale
Taxi driver	John Harmon
Eddie	Ben Welden
John	John Ridgely
John Dill	Cliff Clark
Gatekeeper	Arthur Aylesworth
Captain Strong	Matthew Boulton
Captain Hunter	Gavin Muir
Ralph Bryon	Frank M. Thomas
Carl	James Seay
Joe	Charles Drake
Miller	Murray Alper

Synopsis:

Dr. Michael Lewis, a handsome young interne, becomes involved with Jane, whom he helps after an accident. She claims to be a British secret agent, and pleads with Lewis to help her escape the men accompanying her, explaining that they are German spies. Lewis does not believe her, thinking she is simply upset after her near brush with death in the accident. However, after hearing and seeing two of the men, Dr. Ingersoll and Mr. Goodwin, Lewis's suspicions are aroused. When the opportunity arises, he helps Jane escape and learns of a secret fleet of German U-Boats waiting off the coast of the United States. Jane and the young doctor flee the German agents and try desperately to get someone to believe their story and help. Eventually they find aid, and the U-Boat fleet is destroyed and the Nazi fifth columnists are killed or captured.

Reviews:

Philip T. Hartung in *Commonweal:*

"'Dangerously They Live' brings up the espionage-nazi agent aspect of the war again — an aspect that Hollywood has practically worn out with over-coverage . . . . Everyone lives dangerously indeed under Robert Florey's cinema-wise direction."

Bosley Crowther in the *New York Times:*

"With little more finesse than the Gang Busters normally employ, the Warner Brothers are off on another spy-catching chase in an item called 'Dangerously They Live' . . . . Anyone who has watched a previous Warner pursuit, whether the villains were spies or just plain, old-fashioned racketeers, can pretty well call the turns in this not even remotely subtle film . . . . John Garfield, the rough-and-ready glamour boy, plays the single-handed hero in this instance with cool and square-jawed conviction. And Nancy Coleman, an engaging newcomer, provokes much interest as the distraught British girl. 'Dangerously They Live' is purest pretense, but it manages to hide its shoddy rather well."

Note:

Dangerously They Live opened at the Strand Theatre in New York on April 10, 1942.

Filming a scene with Nancy Coleman.

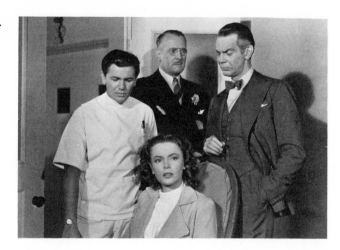

With Moroni Olsen, Raymond Massey, Nancy Coleman.

*With Moroni Olsen, Raymond Massey, Nancy Coleman,
James Seay, John Ridgely, Ilka Gruning.*

With Nancy Coleman.

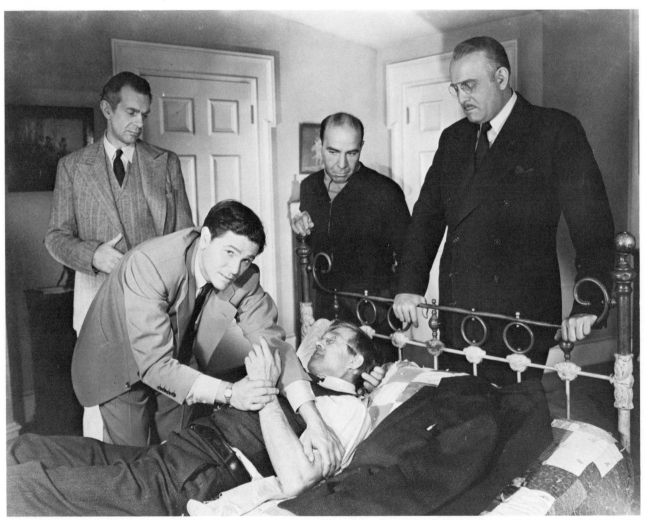

With Raymond Massey, Christian Rub, Ben Welden, Moroni Olsen.

15
Tortilla Flat
1942

Credits:

A Metro-Goldwyn-Mayer Production. Directed by Victor Fleming. Produced by Sam Zimbalist. Screenplay by John Lee Mahin and Benjamin Glazer. Based on the novel by John Steinbeck. Director of photography, Karl Freund. Music by Franz Waxman. Film editor, James E. Newcom. Art director, Cedric Gibbons. Special effects by Warren Newcombe. Musical lyrics by Frank Loesser. Running time, 105 minutes.

Cast:

Pilon	Spencer Tracy
Dolores Sweets Ramirez	Hedy Lamarr
Danny	John Garfield
The Pirate	Frank Morgan
Pablo	Akim Tamiroff
Tito Ralph	Sheldon Leonard
Jose Maria Corcoran	John Qualen
Paul D. Cummings	Donald Meek
Mrs. Torelli	Connie Gilchrist
Portagee Joe	Allen Jenkins
Father Ramon	Henry O'Neill
Mrs. Marellis	Mercedes Ruffino
Senora Teresina	Nina Campana
Mr. Brown	Arthur Space
Cesca	Betty Wells
Torrelli	Harry Burns

Synopsis:

In Tortilla Flat, a ramshackle area in a poor California coastal fishing village, a group of itinerant loafers, *paisanos*, while away their time drinking, brawling, loving, and avoiding work. One of them, Danny, receives an inheritance when his grandfather dies. The inheritance consists of two clapboard houses and a gold watch. Now a man of property, Danny feels very important, and his romance with Dolores Sweets Ramirez suddenly blooms. His friends, Pilon, Pablo, Tito, and Jose Maria, fear that all Dolores is interested in is his houses. They set about to forestall the upcoming marriage. Pilon steals Danny's watch and hocks it for four jugs of wine, and inadvertently burns down one of Danny's houses.

Meanwhile, Pirate, a bearded old fellow who lives with five dogs, is saving up one thousand "two-bitses" in order to buy a golden candlestick for St. Francis. His friends try to steal it, again for wine money, until they find out what the money is for. Pirate says he had seen St. Francis in a vision and was told, "Be good to dogs, you dirty man." Pirate then took in a lot of dogs and discovered their steady friendship. In gratitude, he wants to buy a candlestick for the saint. After buying it and taking it to the church, he takes his dogs into the woods and describes the ceremony to them in detail.

Danny decides to do the unthinkable and get a job in order to make up the price of the lost house and marry Dolores. They marry and, while the couple is honeymooning, the *paisanos* resign themselves to the situation and sorrowfully burn down Danny's other house.

Reviews:

Manny Farber in the *New Republic:*

"John Garfield and Spencer Tracy play Danny and Pilon in the hard-boiled tradition of Sergeant Quirt, replete with Brooklyn accent, and whenever Hedy Lamarr opens her mouth the wrong words with the wrong feeling invariably come out. Victor Fleming directs in a kind of dreary conservatism that doesn't turn up one emotion in eighty minutes."

Philip T. Hartung in *Commonweal:*

"Victor Fleming has done an excellent job of directing his characters. John Garfield plays Danny to perfection, giving full justification for all the promise he exhibited several years ago when he first stepped into films."

John Mosher in *The New Yorker:*

As a gypsy leader, Spencer Tracy may be a bit too magisterial, heavy-shouldered, and broad-browed. Hedy Lamarr and John Garfield have no trouble with the problems of innocent amour, the noisy misunderstanding of a great passion in an ideal climate, and swing through the paces with considerable zest. There is clearly a charm about the whole affair."

Newsweek:

"While the story offers little action, Victor Fleming, the director, makes the most of its atmosphere and ingratiating attitudes, and an exceptionally strong cast. The result is an unusual film that creates a reasonable facsimile of the Steinbeck flavor."

Time:

"Steinbeck's *paisanos* were shiftless, harmless, simple, brawling, wine-bibbing Mexican mixed-breeds; M-G-M's are purebreds Spencer Tracy, Frank Morgan, John Garfield, et al. It is hard for them to be *paisanos,* but Victor Fleming's eloquent direction produces many a memorable sequence from the formless, wandering story."

Notes:

Tortilla Flat was the first film Garfield made for a studio other than Warners. Co-star Frank Morgan won an Oscar nomination for best supporting actor for his role as Pirate, but lost to Van Heflin for his part in *Johnny Eager.*

Tortilla Flat opened at Radio City Music Hall in New York on May 21 1942.

With Spencer Tracy.

With Spencer Tracy, Akim Tamiroff, Sheldon Leonard.

With Allen Jenkins, John Qualen, a player, Spencer Tracy, Akim Tamiroff.

With Frank Morgan, John Qualen, Spencer Tracy. Allen Jenkins, Akim Tamiroff.

With Spencer Tracy, Hedy Lamarr.

With Sheldon Leonard, Akim Tamiroff, Spencer Tracy.

16
Air Force
1943

Credits:

A Warner Bros.-First National Picture. Directed by Howard Hawks. Produced by Hal B. Wallis. Original screenplay by Dudley Nichols. Director of photography, James Wong Howe. Music by Franz Waxman. Film editor, George Amy. Dialogue director, William Faulkner. Assistant director, Jack Sullivan. Art director, John Hughes. Special effects by Roy Davidson, Rex Wimpy, and H. F. Koenekamp. Sound recorder, Oliver S. Garretson. Orchestrations by Leo F. Forbstein. Aerial photography by Elmer Dyer and Charles Marshall. Chief pilot, Paul Mantz. Set decoration by Walter F. Tilford. Running time, 124 minutes.

Cast:

Capt. Quincannon	John Ridgely
Sgt. Winocki	John Garfield
Sgt. White	Harry Carey
Lieut. Williams	Gig Young
Lieut. McMartin	Arthur Kennedy
Lieut. Hauser	Charles Drake
Cpl. Weinberg	George Tobias
Cpl. Peterson	Ward Wood
Pvt. Chester	Ray Montgomery
Lieut. Rader	James Brown
Maj. Mallory	Stanley Ridges
Colonel	Willard Robertson
Commanding officer	Moroni Olsen
Sgt. Callahan	Edward Brophy
Maj. Roberts	Richard Lane
Lieut. Moran	Bill Crago
Susan McMartin	Faye Emerson
Maj. Daniels	Addison Richards
Maj. Bagley	James Flavin
Mary Quincannon	Ann Doran
Mrs. Chester	Dorothy Peterson
Marine with dog	James Millican
Cmdr. Harper	William Forrest
Demolition corporal	Murray Alper
Officer at Hickam Field	George Neise
Marine	Tom Neal
Quincannon's son	Henry Blair
Control Officer	Warren Douglas
Nurse	Ruth Ford
2nd nurse	Leah Baird
Sergeants	Bill Hopper
	Sol Gorss
2nd control officer	James Bush
Ground crewman	George Offerman, Jr.
Joe	Walter Sande
Nurses	Lynne Baggett
	Marjorie Hoshelle
1st Lieutenant	Theodore von Eltz
2nd Lieutenant	Ross Ford
Copilot	Rand Brooks

Synopsis:

The *Mary Ann,* with eight other B-17 Flying Fortresses, takes off from California on a routine training flight to Hawaii on December 6, 1941. Aboard are the pilot, Capt. Quincannon, a young veteran of the Texas training fields, crew chief Sgt. White, Cpl. Weinberg, radio operators Cpl. Peterson and Pvt. Chester, and Lt. Hauser, the navigator. Other members of the crew include copilot Lt. Williams, McMartin, the bombardier, and the aerial gunner, Sgt. Winocki.

En route, they receive the news of the Japanese attack on Pearl Harbor and their destination, Hickam Field. They land instead on Maui, where they are attacked by fifth columnists. They escape, and soon receive orders to fly to Wake Island. During their half-hour stop on Wake, they pick up a pursuit pilot, Lt. Rader, who is needed in Manila. Shortly after landing at Clark Field in Manila, they are involved in a Japanese attack on the field. Ordered to head for Australia, the *Mary Ann* and her sleepless crew go up for a crack at some Japanese ships first. Attacked by Japanese Zeros, the *Mary Ann* is badly damaged. Capt. Quincannon, seriously wounded, orders the crew to bail out. All do so but Winocki, who, trained but washed out as a pilot, takes over the controls and brings the ship back to the field.

The crew of the *Mary Ann* works all night trying to patch her up for flying with parts from other wrecked ships. Ordered to destroy her, the men promise to get the ship into the air or to burn her before the Japanese arrive. Quincannon dies and Rader takes over. Heading for Australia, the *Mary Ann* sights an enemy task force and takes part in the Coral Sea battle. Riddled with bullets, the *Mary Ann* crashes and burns on an Australian beach. The crew gets out and finds a new B-17 waiting for them at the Australian base. They name her the *Mary Ann II.*

Reviews:

Philip T. Hartung in *Commonweal:*

"When Warner Brothers decided to produce 'Air Force,' they must have decided to make a flying film that was bigger and better than all others. They have done just that.... If 'Air Force' were 30 minutes shorter it would be not only 'bigger' but 'best'. As it is, it is bigger and very good."

Manny Farber in *The New Republic:*

"It is the best, most interesting, movie record to date of the Pacific war theatre.... Of the players, John Ridgely has the tall, unbothered efficiency and respectable good looks of a pilot or a bus driver ... the soft, goodlooking Southern aviator that used to be Johnny Mack Brown is now capably and graciously James Brown."

David Larner in *The New Yorker:*

"The most irresistible personalities involved are John Garfield and Harry Carey, who appear to be perfectly content to speak when spoken to."

"*Air Force,* a superbly thrilling show, is easily the best aviation film to date."

Bosley Crowther in the *New York Times:*

"It is ... a continuously fascinating, frequently thrilling and occasionally exalting show which leaves you limp and triumphant at the end of its two-hour ordeal.... John Ridgely is refreshingly direct as the bomber's intrepid captain and sufficiently unfamiliar to seem real. Harry Carey gives a beautiful performance as the quiet and efficient crew chief, and John Garfield's tough creation of Winocki is superior despite its brevity."

Notes:

Air Force figured in the *New York Times* Ten Best Films of 1943, and placed third in the National Board of Review Ten Best. Among the top grossers of 1943, the film won for George Amy the Best Film Editing Oscar.

Air Force opened at the Hollywood Theatre in New York on February 4, 1943.

With John Ridgely.

With George Tobias, Harry Carey, Ward Wood.

A WARNER BROS. PICTURE

Air Force

With Gig Young, Ward Wood.

With Charles Drake, Gig Young, Harry Carey, Murray Alper, Moroni Olsen, George Tobias.

With Harry Carey, Charles Drake, player.

17
The Fallen Sparrow
1943

Credits:

An RKO-Radio Picture. Directed by Richard Wallace. Produced by Robert Fellows. Screenplay by Warren Duff. Based on the novel by Dorothy B. Hughes. Director of photography, Nicholas Musuraca. Music by Roy Webb. Film editor, Robert Wise. Assistant director, Sam Ruman. Art director, Albert S. D'Agostino and Mark-Lee Kirk. Set decorations by Darrell Silvera and Harley Miller. Gowns by Edward Stevenson. Special effects by Vernon L. Walker. Sound recorder, Bailey Fesler. Rerecorded by James G. Stewart. Orchestrations by C. Bakaleinikoff. Production designed by Van Nest Polglase. Running time, 94 minutes.

Cast:

Kit (John McKittrick)	John Garfield
Toni Donne	Maureen O'Hara
Dr. Skaas	Walter Slezak
Whitney Parker	Martha O'Driscoll
Barby Taviton	Patricia Morison
Anton	John Banner
Inspector Tobin	John Miljan
Otto Skaas	Hugh Beaumont
Prince Francois de Namur	Sam Goldberg
Guest	Symona Boniface

Synopsis:

In November of 1940, John McKittrick arrives in New York, looking for truth behind the "suicide" of his friend Louie Lepetino, a private eye. Having just returned from the Spanish Civil War where he was a prisoner, Kit moves in with his friend Ab Parker. They go to a party where Kit meets Whitney and her pianist Anton, Doctor and Otto Skaas, and Toni Donne, the granddaughter of Prince de Namur. Whitney tells Kit about Louie's death at a similar party and that she suspects the Skaas brothers of being Nazi agents. At home, Kit finds Louie's wallet and a note he had sent Louie from prison, which someone has obviously planted in Kit's overcoat. Kit has nightmares involving the torture he underwent in Spain and the limping footsteps of his Nazi torturer.

Later, after trying and failing to make a date with Toni, Kit tells Whitney about his experiences in Spain. He tells her that he is being chased by a Nazi who wants a Spanish battle flag that Kit possesses and cannot give up. Toni finally agrees to go out with Kit, and she reveals that she planted Louie's wallet and that Kit has been watched since his arrival. That night Kit is jumped by Anton, whom he subdues and questions. Anton tells him that Kit was allowed to escape from prison in order that the Nazi could follow him to the flag's location. Kit throws Anton out and goes to bed. In the morning he wakes up to find Ab murdered. Kit's friend Inspector Tobin arrives and announces that Ab's death was suicide. Later, however, Tobin tells Kit that he is aware of the true situation, but had to keep him in the dark until he was sure Kit would not crack under the strain. He also tells Kit that Louie had been working for the government, as had been Ab. Kit in turn reveals the Nazi's revenge plot to get the flag.

Confronting Toni with the truth about the two deaths, Kit learns that Otto Skaas had murdered Louie. Toni agrees to help Kit. That night, while searching Dr. Skaas's room, Kit hears the limping footsteps that have haunted him nearly to insanity. The door opens and Dr. Skaas limps in. He tells Kit that he murdered Ab, and that he has drugged Kit's drink with truth serum. Kit kills the doctor, then collapses.

When he awakens, Toni refuses to go with Kit because she fears reprisals to her family in Germany. He arranges for her to take a new name and go to Chicago, where he will join her after retrieving the flag from Lisbon. But later, he catches her leaving for Lisbon herself to get the flag. Facing up to her lies, he has her arrested and leaves for Lisbon alone.

Reviews:
David Lardner in *The New Yorker:*
"The picture, while it has a fairly high content of hokum, does have points in its favor. One is the information, picked up somewhere, no doubt, by the agents of RKO, that Nazi Germans were running Franco's war. Another is its rather novel ending, a little reminiscent of 'The Maltese Falcon.'"

Theodore Strauss in the *New York Times:*
"By virtue of a taut performance by John Garfield in the central role, and the singular skill with which director Richard Wallace has highlighted the significant climaxes, 'The Fallen Sparrow' emerges as one of the uncommon and provocatively handled melodramas of recent months . . . . Through these scenes Mr. Garfield remains almost constantly convincing and without his sure and responsive performance in a difficult role Mr. Wallace's effects would have been lost entirely."

Notes:
The Fallen Sparrow features sinister performances by two actors later famed for genial roles: John Banner, who gained weight and reknown in the role of Schultz on TV's "Hogan's Heroes," and Hugh Beaumont, famous as the wise father on the "Leave It to Beaver" series. The film was edited by Robert Wise, long before his direction of *The Sound of Music* and *The Sand Pebbles*.

The Fallen Sparrow opened at the Palace Theatre in New York on August 19, 1943.

With Symona Boniface, Walter Slezak, Maureen O'Hara.

With John Banner, Martha O'Driscoll, player.

With Patricia Morison.

With Walter Slezak.

With John Miljan.

18
Show Business at War
1943

Credits:

A Twentieth Century-Fox production. Volume IX, Issue 10 of *The March of Time.* Directed by Louis deRochement. Produced by the editors of *Time* magazine. Running time, 17 minutes.

Cast:

As Themselves

Eddie "Rochester" Anderson, Louis Armstrong, Phil Baker, Ethel Barrymore, Robert Benchley, Jack Benny, Edgar Bergen, Irving Berlin, Joe E. Brown, James Cagney, Bing Crosby, Michael Curtiz, Linda Darnell, Bette Davis, Olivia de Havilland, Marlene Dietrich, Walt Disney, Irene Dunne, Deanna Durbin, W.C. Fields, Errol Flynn, Glenn Ford, Kay Francis, Clark Gable, John Garfield, Bert Glennon, Rita Hayworth, Alfred Hitchcock, Bob Hope, Al Jolson, Brenda Joyce, Kay Kyser, Hedy Lamarr, Dorothy Lamour, Carole Landis, Gertrude Lawrence, Anatole Litvak, Carole Lombard, Myrna Loy, Alfred Lunt, Fred MacMurray, Victor Mature, Mitzi Mayfair, the Mills Brothers, George Murphy, Eugene Ormandy, Tyrone Power, the Ritz Brothers, Ginger Rogers, Mickey Rooney, Frank Sinatra, Greg Toland, Lana Turner, Hal Wallis, Jack Warner, Orson Welles, Loretta Young, Darryl Zanuck.

Note:

Show Business at War was a multistudio effort for the *March of Time* newsreel. It gathered many stars in a gala attempt to show the progress of the Hollywood war effort.

19
Thank Your Lucky Stars
1943

Credits:

A Warner Bros.-First National Picture. Directed by David Butler. Produced by Mark Hellinger. Screenplay by Norman Panama, Melvin Frank, and James V. Kern. Based on a story by Everett Freeman and Arthur Schwartz. Director of photography, Arthur Edeson. Music and lyrics by Arthur Schwartz and Frank Loesser. Film editor, Irene Morra. Dialogue director, Herbert Farjean. Assistant director, Phil Quinn. Art directors, Anton Grot and Leo Kuter. Gowns by Milo Anderson. Makeup artist, Perc Westmore. Special effects by H. F. Koenekamp. Sound recorders, Francis J. Scheid and Charles David Forrest. Orchestrations by Leo F. Forbstein. Dances created and staged by LeRoy Prinz. Orchestral arrangements by Ray Heindorf. Vocal arrangements by Dudley Chambers. Musical adaptation by Heinz Roemheld. Additional orchestrations by Maurice de Packh. Running time, 124 minutes.

Cast:

Himself and Joe Simpson	Eddie Cantor
Pat Dixon	Joan Leslie
Tom Randolph	Dennis Morgan
Farnsworth	Edward Everett Horton
Dr. Schlenna	S.Z. Sakall
Nurse Hamilton	Ruth Donnelly
Announcer	Don Wilson
Barber	Henry Armetta
Assistant photographer	Hank Mann
Fan	Mary Treen
Bill	James Burke
Dr. Kirby	Paul Harvey
Patient	Bert Gordon
Drunk	Jack Norton
Jitterbug	Conrad Wiedell
Fireman	Matt McHugh
Sailor	Frank Faylen
Charlie	Noble Johnson
Olaf	Mike Mazurki
Girl with book	Joyce Reynolds
Barney Johnson	Richard Lane
Finchley	William Haade
Pete	Don Barclay
Boy	Stanley Clements
Gossip	Hattie McDaniel
Soldier	Willie Best
Ice Cold Katie	Rita Christiani
Justice	Jess Lee Brooks
Trio	Ford, Harris & Jones
Dancers	Alexis Smith
	Igor DeNaurotsky
	Arnold Kent
Cabdriver	Brandon Hurst
Miss Latin America	Lynne Baggett
Miss Spain	Mary Landa
Himself	Humphrey Bogart
Herself	Bette Davis
Herself	Olivia De Havilland
Himself	Errol Flynn
Himself	John Garfield

Herself	Ida Lupino
Herself	Ann Sheridan
Herself	Dinah Shore
Herself	Alexis Smith
Himself	Jack Carson
Himself	Alan Hale
Himself	George Tobias
Himself	David Butler
Himself	Mark Hellinger
Themselves	Spike Jones and His City Slickers

with

Monte Blue, Art Foster, Fred Kelsey, Elmer Ballard, Buster Wiles, Howard Davies, Tudor Williams, Alan Cook, Fred McEvoy, Bobby Hale, Will Stanton, Charles Irwin, David Thursby, Henry Iblings, Earl Hunsaker, Hubert Head, Dudley Kuzelle, Ted Billings.

Synopsis:

Eddie Cantor insists upon being chairman of Farnsworth and Schlenna's Cavalcade of Stars benefit, in return for the use of his vocalist, Dinah Shore. Cantor takes over the rehearsals and destroys the producers' plans. Meanwhile, singer Tom Randolph and songwriter Pat Dixon, chasing a crooked agent who sold them phony contracts, discover Joe Simpson, a bus driver who would like to act, but can't because he too closely resembles Eddie Cantor. They decide to have Cantor kidnapped, and to have Joe replace him, thus giving them all a chance in the show. Cantor escapes his captors and rushes to the theatre, but Joe convinces everyone that Cantor is an impostor. Cantor is thrown out, and Joe leads the show to success.

Reviews:

Philip T. Hartung in *Commonweal:*

"The outstanding thing about "Thank Your Lucky Stars" is not what its stars do, but that they do it. Warner Brothers has gathered its leading performers and put them through some square hoops . . . . The fans might eat it up. I'll take vanilla."

Newsweek:

"Despite the time, talent, and expense that went into this musical, its moments of first-rate showmanship are all too rare; the general atmosphere is that of the talented, if not-quite-professional varsity show."

Time:

"The picture is most amusing as a sort of glorified Amateur Night."

Bosley Crowther in the *New York Times:*

"John Garfield is highly amusing singing a tough guy's version of "Blues in the Night" . . . . It is also too much [two hours] of a show. But, in straight omnibus entertainment that's what you have to expect."

Notes:

Most of the Warner contract players of the time appeared in *Thank Your Lucky Stars,* which was one of the top-grossing films of 1943. The storyline is weak, and really it is only an excuse to get everyone on the Warner lot into one picture.

Thank Your Lucky Stars opened at the Strand Theatre in New York on October 1, 1943.

20
Destination Tokyo
1944

Credits:

A Warner Bros. Picture. Directed by Delmer Daves. Produced by Jerry Wald. Screenplay by Delmer Daves and Albert Maltz. Based on a story by Steve Fisher. Director of photography, Bert Glennon. Music by Franz Waxman. Film editor, Christian Nyby. Assistant director, Art Lueker. Art director, Leo Kuter. Set decoration by Walter Tilford. Costumes by Vladimir Barjansky. Special effects by Lawrence Butler and Willard Van Enger. Sound recorder, Robert B. Lee. Orchestrations by Leo F. Forbstein. Narrated by Lou Marcelle. Technical advisor, Lt. Cmdr. Phillip Compson. Running time, 135 minutes.

Cast:

Capt. Cassidy	Cary Grant
Wolf	John Garfield
Cookie	Alan Hale
Reserve officer	John Ridgely
Tin Can	Dane Clark
Executive officer	Warner Anderson
Pills	William Prince
The Kid	Robert Hutton
Dakota	Peter Whitney
Mike	Tom Tully
Mrs. Cassidy	Faye Emerson
Diving officer	Warren Douglas
Sparks	John Forsythe
Ensign	John Alvin
Ensign	Ralph McColm
Torpedo Gunnery officer	Bill Kennedy
C.O.	John Whitney
Quartermaster	William Challee
YoYo	Whit Bissell
Chief of Boat	George Lloyd
Toscanini	Maurice Murphy
Admiral	Pierre Watkin
Aide	Stephen Richards (Mark Stevens)
Hornet's Admiral	Cliff Clark
Debby Cassidy	Deborah Daves
Michael Cassidy	Michael Daves
Aide	Jack Mower
Tin Can's girl	Mary Landa
Man on phone	Carlyle Blackwell
Captain	Kirby Grant
C.P.O.	Lane Chandler
Wolf's girl	Joy Barlowe
Market Street "commando"	Bill Hunter
Crewmen	George Robotham
	Dan Borzage
	William Hudson
	Charles Sullivan
	Duke York
	Harry Bartell
	Jay Ward
	Paul Langton

Synopsis:

The U.S.S. *Copperfin* leaves San Francisco Bay

December 24, 1942 under sealed orders. Once out to sea, Captain Cassidy opens the orders and announces their goal — Tokyo. In the Aleutians, an American plane delivers a weather expert to the *Copperfin.* Before the sub can submerge, it is spotted by a Japanese plane. The plane attacks and is shot down, but not before a bomb goes through the aft deck without exploding. Cassidy orders the Japanese pilot picked up. The pilot stabs the sailor helping him aboard and is subsequently killed by another sailor.

The sub eventually reaches Tokyo Bay. There it waits outside the mine fields and submarine nets until a Jap cruiser is escorted through the barriers. The *Copperfin* follows along, submerged and undetected. Then the real mission is unfolded. The reserve officer and two other sailors are put ashore in a remote area. They make weather observations and spot varied strategic points, radioing the information to waiting forces of General Doolittle's bombing team. Japanese soldiers locate the broadcasting station and attack, but the Americans escape to the *Copperfin.* While submerged in Tokyo Bay, one sailor comes down with appendicitis, and the pharmacist's mate performs an emergency operation.

As Doolittle's bombers raid Tokyo, a Japanese carrier escapes, thereby opening the harbor exit for the *Copperfin.* The sub sinks the carrier and a destroyer, and sails back to San Francisco.

Reviews:

David Lardner in *The New Yorker:*

"Altogether too much happens in 'Destination Tokyo,' a long, long submarine epic.... It's no more lively than a couple of dozen other war pictures.... Incidentally, the picture contains, for your collection, one more kid who's just starting to shave.'

Newsweek:

"Warner Brothers' newest tribute to the armed forces rates very near the top of the list.... Cary Grant gives one of the soundest performances of his career; and John Garfield, William Prince, Dane Clark, and the rest of the all-male cast are always credible either as ordinary human beings or extraordinary heroes."

Bosley Crowther in the *New York Times:*

"The Warners have got a pippin of a submarine action film in 'Destination Tokyo,' which came to the Strand yesterday. Mind you, we don't say it's authentic.... Delmar Daves directed and helped write the script with Albert Maltz. Credit all and sundry with the first thundering war film of the year."

Notes:

Destination Tokyo was a top-grossing film for 1944, and made that year's *New York Times* Ten Best List. Scenes from the film are seen in 1951's John Wayne sub-epic *Operation Pacific.*

With Joy Barlowe, Bill Hunter.

With Cary Grant, John Forsythe, Alan Hale, Peter Whitney,
Tom Tully, William Prince, Robert Hutton, crewmen.

121

With Alan Hale, Peter Whitney, Cary Grant, Warner
Anderson, Robert Hutton, Warren Douglas, John Ridgely,
Dane Clark on the Warner lot.

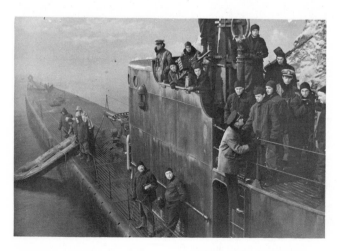

With Alan Hale, Peter Whitney, Cary Grant, Warner
Anderson, John Ridgely, Robert Hutton, Warrne Douglas,
Dane Clark, Tom Tully, William Challee, crewmen.

With Dane Clark, Cary Grant, Robert Hutton, Warren Douglas, crewmen.

21
Between Two Worlds
1944

Credits:

A Warner Bros. Picture. Directed by Edward A. Blatt. Produced by Mark Hellinger. Screenplay by Daniel Fuchs. Based on the play *Outward Bound*, by Sutton Vane. Director of photography, Carl Guthrie. Music by Erich Wolfgang Korngold. Film editor, Rudy Fehr. Dialogue director, Frederick De Cordova. Assistant director, Elmer Decker. Art director, Hugh Reticker. Set decoration by Jack McConaghy. Gowns by Leah Rhodes. Makeup by Perc Westmore. Sound recorder, Clare A. Riggs. Orchestrations by Leo F. Forbstein. Running time, 112 minutes.

Cast:

Tom Prior	John Garfield
Henry	Paul Henreid
Thompson	Sydney Greenstreet
Ann	Eleanor Parker
Scrubby	Edmund Gwenn
Pete Musick	George Tobias
Lingley	George Coulouris
Maxine	Faye Emerson
Mrs. Midget	Sara Allgood
Rev. William Duke	Dennis King
Mr. Cliveden-Banks	Gilbert Emery
Mrs. Cliveden-Banks	Isobel Elsom
Dispatcher	Lester Matthews
Clerk	Pat O'Moore

Synopsis:

Several people are killed in a London air raid as they are going to a ship taking them to safety. The ship becomes their transport to heaven or hell. Aboard are Tom Prior, a derelict newsman, Maxine, a faded showgirl, Cliveden-Banks and his society snob wife, American merchant seaman Pete Musick, and Rev. William Duke. Also among them are Mrs. Midget, a meek little housekeeper, and Lingley, the arrogant head of Lingley, Ltd.

Austrian pianist Henry and his wife Ann almost miss the ship. They did not die in the air raid, but committed suicide by turning on the gas in their rooms. Scrubby, the ship's steward, tells them that they alone know they are dead because their deaths were by choice. But before much time passes, all of the ship's passengers realize exactly what their situation is.

The passengers are visited and interviewed by Thompson, the Examiner, who tells each of them their fates. Mrs. Midget rejects her heavenly reward in order to accompany Tom Prior on his second chance on the hard road of redemption when he is revealed to be her lost son.

Henry is required to travel on the ship forever while Ann goes to heaven. But she insists on staying with him. Scrubby pleads with the Examiner to allow this. Henry despairingly walks out of the room, with Ann following. They find themselves back in London with the gas swept out of their room through a broken window. They are alive.

Reviews:

Newsweek:

"In attempting to bring Vane's spirit world up to date, Daniel Fuchs has merely obscured its persuasive simplicity with topical references and dialogue that is either pompous or pedestrian. The cast is left pretty much at loose ends by Edward Blatt's direction and the revised material at hand."

Bosley Crowther in the *New York Times:*

" . . . this production is competent, though the script runs entirely to discourse, and Director Edward A. Blatt has managed to move his people around with some pain. The performances are generally satisfactory. Paul Henreid and Eleanor Parker are very good as the sadly romantic 'half way' couple. Edmund Gwenn makes a lovable steward and Sydney Greenstreet is amiably rigid as the ultimate Examiner. John Garfield is somewhat too splashy as the broken-down newspaperman, and his popular talent for 'tough' roles makes his casting in this dubious."

Time:

"Nearly all the parts are well played, though as individuals and as moral and social symbols, the characters seem over-genteel, stagily conceived, dated . . . . This older mixed metaphor of death seems all but inspired."

Notes:

Between Two Worlds is a remake of the 1930 *Outward Bound,* which starred Leslie Howard in the Garfield role, although Howard had played the Henreid part in the Broadway play.

Between Two Worlds opened at the Strand Theatre in New York on May 5, 1944.

With Faye Emerson.

With George Tobias, George Coulouris, Paul Henreid, Sara Allgood.

With Faye Emerson.

126

With Paul Henreid, George Tobias.

With Paul Henreid, Eleanor Parker.

22
Hollywood Canteen
1944

Credits:

A Warner Bros.-First National Picture. Directed by Delmer Daves. Produced by Alex Gottlieb. Original screenplay by Delmer Daves. Director of Photography, Bert Glennon. Music by Ray Heindorf. Film editor, Christian Nyby. Assistant director, Art Luker. Art director, Leo Kuter. Costumes by Milo Anderson. Makeup artist, Perc Westmore. Sound recorders, Oliver S. Garretson and Charles David Forrest. Orchestrations by Leo F. Forbstein. Musical numbers created and directed by LeRoy Prinz. Sets by Casey Roberts. Unit manager, Chuck Hanson. Running time, 124 minutes.

Cast:

Joan	Joan Leslie
Slim	Robert Hutton
Sergeant	Dane Clark
Angela	Janis Paige
Mr. Brodel	Jonathan Hale
Mrs. Brodel	Barbara Brown
Soldier on deck	Dick Erdman
Soldier on deck	Steve Richards (Mark Stevens)
Marine sergeant	James Flavin
Dance director	Eddie Marr
Director	Theodore von Eltz
Captain	Ray Teal
Orchestra leader	Rudolph Friml, Jr.

Dancers	Betty Bryson
	Willard Van Simmons
	William Alcorn
	Jack Mattis
	Jack Coffey
Tough Marine	George Turner
Themselves	The Andrews Sisters
Himself	Jack Benny
Himself	Joe E. Brown
Himself	Eddie Cantor
Herself	Kitty Carlisle
Himself	Jack Carson
Herself	Joan Crawford
Himself	Helmut Dantine
Herself	Bette Davis
Herself	Faye Emerson
Himself	Victor Francen
Himself	John Garfield
Himself	Sydney Greenstreet
Himself	Alan Hale
Himself	Paul Henreid
Herself	Andrea King
Himself	Peter Lorre
Herself	Ida Lupino
Himself	Dennis Morgan
Herself	Eleanor Parker
Himself	William Prince
Himself	John Ridgely
Themselves	Roy Rogers & Trigger
Himself	S. Z. Sakall
Himself	Zachary Scott
Herself	Alexis Smith
Herself	Barbara Stanwyck
Himself	Craig Stevens

Himself	Joseph Szigeti
Himself	Donald Woods
Herself	Jane Wyman
Themselves	Jimmy Dorsey & His Orchestra
Themselves	Carmen Cavallaro & His Orchestra
Themselves	The Golden Gate Quartet
Themselves	Rosario & Antonio
Themselves	The Sons of the Pioneers
Herself	Irene Manning
Herself	Nora Martin
Herself	Joan McCracken
Herself	Dolores Moran
Herself	Joyce Reynolds
Herself	Virginia Patton
Herself	Lynne Baggett
Herself	Betty Alexander
Herself	Julie Bishop
Himself	Robert Shayne

with

Johnny Mitchell, John Sheridan, Colleen Townsend, Angela Green, Paul Brooke, Marianne O'Brien, Dorothy Malone, Bill Kennedy, Mary Gordon, Chef Joseph Milani, and Betty Brodel.

Synopsis:

Slim and Sergeant, on sick leave before returning to duty in New Guinea, visit the famed Hollywood Canteen, and Slim becomes the millionth G.I. to enter its doors. As his prize, he wins a date with Joan Leslie, while Sergeant gets to dance with Joan Crawford. They listen to Canteen President Bette Davis and Vice-President John Garfield review the Canteen's past, and enjoy musical entertainment by many stars.

Reviews:

W.G. in *The New Yorker:*

"'Hollywood Canteen,' while clearly virtuous in purpose, is certainly one of the most majestic bores ever imposed on the American people."

Newsweek:

"Delmer Daves, who wrote 'Stage Door Canteen' for Sol Lesser last year, does it again with minor changes for Warner Brothers' 'Hollywood Canteen.' The difference between the two films is strictly geographical .... The final effect is that of a giant benefit show."

Time:

"As a grab bag of short turns, encores and gracious gestures by well-liked Warner names (Dennis Morgan, Jack Benny, John Garfield, Bette Davis, Jane Wyman, S.Z. Sakall) and name bands (Jimmy Dorsey, Carmen Cavallaro), *Hollywood Canteen* is pleasant enough until it becomes plethoric."

Bosley Crowther in the *New York Times:*

"If it's quantity you want in entertainment — entertainment, that is, of the sort that is generally thrown together in an "all-star benefit show" — then Warners' grotesquely laden 'Hollywood Canteen' is for you .... But if it's quality you want in your entertainment and just a slight touch of dramatic grace, beware the elaborate hocus-pocus of 'Hollywood Canteen.' There is not a fairly distinguished song or turn of dialogue in the show, and the story which binds the 'acts' together is an embarrassingly affected affair.... In a more or less introductory comment, Joe E. Brown describes Hollywood Canteen: 'This place is just a great big juke box.' So is the film. It is that full of stuff."

Notes:

Hollywood Canteen ranked as one of 1945's top-grossing films. Garfield, who co-founded the Canteen with Bette Davis, tells of its history and its works on behalf of American G.I.'s. Scenes from the film are visible in the 1946 Cary Grant picture, *Night and Day.*

Hollywood Canteen opened at the Strand Theatre in New York on December 15, 1944.

With Robert Hutton, Bette Davis.

With Jack Carson, Jane Wyman, Bette Davis, servicemen.

130

With Bette Davis, Joan Leslie.

With Robert Hutton.

23
Pride of the Marines
1945

Credits:

A Warner Bros. Picture. Directed by Delmer Daves. Produced by Jerry Wald. Screenplay by Albert Maltz. Adapted by Marvin Borowsky from a book by Roger Butterfield. Director of photography, Peverall Marley. Music by Franz Waxman. Film editor, Owen Marks. Orchestrations by Leo F. Forbstein and Leonid Raab. Running time, 120 minutes.

Cast:

Al Schmid	John Garfield
Ruth Hartley	Eleanor Parker
Lee Diamond	Dane Clark
Jim Merchant	John Ridgely
Virginia Pfeiffer	Rosemary DeCamp
Ella Merchant	Ann Doran
Lucy Merchant	Ann Todd
Kebabian	Warren Douglas
Irish	Don McGuire
Tom	Tom D'Andrea
Doctor	Rory Mallinson
Ainslee	Steven Richards
Johnny Rivers	Anthony Caruso
Captain Burroughs	Moroni Olsen

with

Dave Willock, John Sheridan, John Miles, John Campton, Lennie Bremen, and Michael Browne.

Synopsis:

Al Schmid joins the U.S. Marine Corps after Pearl Harbor, primarily because he thinks "shooting Japs would be more fun than shooting bear." On Guadalcanal during a night attack, hordes of Japanese soldiers cross the Tenaru River dividing them from Al's machine-gun nest. Al and his buddies, Lee Diamond and Johnny Rivers, hold off the enemy, but Johnny is killed and Al is blinded by a grenade.

In a U.S. hospital, Al dictates letters to his girl, Ruth, at first deceiving her about his sight. Later he tries to break with her, fearing that he will become a burden. His doctor tells Al that he may never see again, but Al refuses to believe him and declines to study Braille. Unwillingly brought home to Philadelphia, Al still fears marriage. His friend Lee tries to explain that many people are handicapped in many ways, describing his own difficulty in getting work because he is a Jew. Unconvinced, Al tries to leave during a Christmas party, but walks into the tree. Now realizing he cannot make his way alone, he marries Ruth, and under her care, he partially regains his sight to the point that he can distinguish shapes and colors.

Reviews:

James Agee in *The Nation:*

"Very good performances by John Garfield and Dane Clark. Long, drawn out and never inspired, but very respectably honest and dogged, thanks considerably, it appears, to Albert Maltz's screenplay."

Manny Farber in *The New Republic:*

"The film is definitely above the current average in every department except that of background music . . . . John Garfield, when he is trying to be anything but hard and defensive and is allowed to talk a little less and at a speed slower than his usual imitation of a drill press, becomes surprisingly boyish, somewhat woebegone, nice-spirited and more valuable as an actor than I have ever seen him be."

W.G. in *The New Yorker:*

"In spite of the fact that most of this has a somewhat familiar and mechanical air, the picture has its effective moments, mostly owing to Mr. Garfield's honest and very intelligent performance."

Time:

"Even when it drags, the screen story of Al Schmid has a compelling doggedness and honesty. The cast, especially Messrs. Garfield and Clark, put it over with a notable absence of affectation. It is a good hard-hitting movie."

Bosley Crowther in the *New York Times:*

"The performances are all unqualifiedly excellent. John Garfield does a brilliant job as Schmid, cocky and self-reliant and full of a calm, commanding pride . . . . To say that this picture is entertaining to a truly surprising degree is an inadequate recommendation. It is inspiring and eloquent of a quality of human courage that millions must try to generate today."

Notes:

Listed among the *New York Times* Ten Best of 1945, *Pride of the Marines* was based on the real-life story of Al Schmid. The film bears no relation to any of the earlier photoplays of the same title.

Pride of the Marines opened at the Strand Theatre in New York on August 24, 1945.

With Eleanor Parker.

With Anthony Caruso, Dane Clark.

With Dane Clark, Anthony Caruso.

With Rory Mallinson, Rosemary DeCamp.

With Rosemary DeCamp.

24
The Postman Always Rings Twice
1946

Credits:

A Metro-Goldwyn-Mayer production. Directed by Tay Garnett. Produced by Carey Wilson. Screenplay by Harry Ruskin and Niven Busch. Based on the novel by James M. Cain. Director of photography, Sidney Wagner. Music by George Basserman. Film editor, George White. Art directors, Cedric Gibbons and Randall Duell. Orchestrations by Ted Duncan. Song by Neil Moret and Richard Whiting. Running time, 113 minutes.

Cast:

Cora Smith	Lana Turner
Frank Chambers	John Garfield
Nick Smith	Cecil Kellaway
Arthur Keats	Hume Cronyn
Kyle Sackett	Leon Ames
Madge Gorland	Audrey Totter
Ezra Liam Kennedy	Alan Reed
Blair	Jeff York
Doctor	Charles Williams
Willie	Cameron Grant
Ben	Wally Cassell
Judge	William Halligan
Judge	Morris Ankrum
Truckdriver	Garry Owen
Nurse	Dorothy Phillips
Doctor	Edward Earle
Picnic manager	Byron Foulger
Matron	Sondra Morgan
Reporter	Dick Crockett
Bailiff	Frank Mayo
Customer	Betty Blythe
John X. McHugh	Joel Friedkin
Headwaiter	Jack Chefe
Telegraph messenger	George Noisom
Snooty woman	Virginia Randolph
Father McConnell	Tom Dillon
Warden	James Farley
Man	Paul Bradley

Synopsis

Nick Smith, the middle-aged proprietor of a roadside restaurant, hires drifter Frank Chambers as a handyman. Frank is immediately attracted to Nick's beautiful wife, Cora. Before long, Cora, who had long before tired of her drab existence, returns his feeling, and they fall in love. Cora hates Nick, and eventually talks Frank into helping her kill him so that they can take over the restaurant. They plan an "accidental" bathroom death, which miscarries. Nick, however, suspects nothing. Frank and Cora then arrange an auto accident by killing Nick, wrecking the car, and leaving evidence that Nick had been drinking. The authorities become suspicious, however, and Frank and Cora are arrested. They are convicted of manslaughter, but receive suspended sentences.

Frank marries Cora, who begins to fear constantly the possibility of being found out. They decide to go away, but are involved in a real auto accident. Cora is killed and Frank is mistakenly charged with her murder. He is convicted and dies in the gas chamber.

Reviews:
James Agee in *The Nation:*

"'The Postman Always Rings Twice' is mainly a terrible misfortune from start to finish. It looks to have been made in a depth of seriousness incompatible with the material, complicated by a paralysis of fear of the front office."

Manny Farber in *The New Republic:*

"The movie, 'The Postman Always Rings Twice,' is almost too terrible to walk out of. The story has been laundered, comicalized, slowed down in the filming, and evidently made by a crew of bobby-sox characters. . . . A lot of Garfield's work slides too easily because he has played a slouching, quizzical roughneck too often."

John McCarten in *The New Yorker:*

"Neither Mr. Garfield nor Miss Turner succeeds entirely in summoning up the violence of disposition called for by the leading roles."

Newsweek:

"Garfield is the right man for his role, and Miss Turner supplies the sex appeal . . . . This long shot can be credited only as a near miss."

Hermine Rich Isaacs in *Theatre Arts:*

"By guiding Miss Turner through her role as a kind of misdirected dove and Mr. Garfield as a muscular fool, they [M-G-M] have failed to recreate the bitter, tawdry, profoundly amoral climate in which such events could only occur."

Bosley Crowther in the *New York Times:*

"'The Postman' . . . comes off a tremendously tense and dramatic show, and it gives Lana Turner and John Garfield the best roles of their careers . . . . Too much cannot be said for the principals. Mr. Garfield reflects to the life the crude and confused young hobo who stumbles aimlessly into a fatal trap. Miss Turner is remarkably effective . . . . "

Notes:

M-G-M bought the rights to the James Cain novel in 1934, but fear of censorship prevented the filming until 1946. It was highly popular, although its sets and costumes, in the M-G-M fashion, were somewhat too glamorous.

The Postman Always Rings Twice opened at the Capitol Theatre in New York on May 2, 1946.

With Lana Turner.

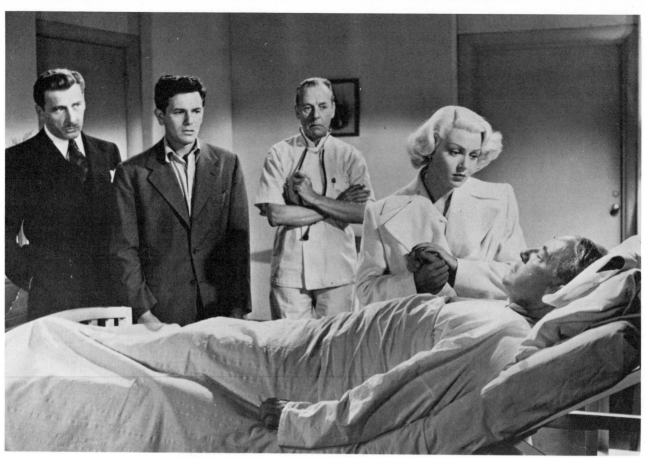

With Leon Ames, Charles Williams, Lana Turner, Cecil Kellaway.

With Cecil Kellaway, Lana Turner.

With Lana Turner.

With Tom Dillon.

139

25
Nobody Lives Forever

1946

Credits:

A Warner Bros.-First National Picture. Directed by Jean Negulesco. Produced by Robert Buckner. Screenplay by W.R. Burnet, based on his novel *I Wasn't Born Yesterday*. Director of photography, Arthur Edeson. Music by Adolph Deutsch. Film editor, Rudi Fehr. Dialogue director, Herschel Daugherty. Assistant director, Reginald Callow. Art director, Hugh Reticker. Set decorations by Casey Roberts. Wardrobe by Milo Anderson. Make-up by Perc Westmore. Special effects by William McGann and Willard Van Enger. Sound recorder, Dolph Thomas. Orchestrations by Jerome Moross. Musical director, Leo F. Forbstein. Running time, 100 minutes.

Cast:

Nick Blake	John Garfield
Gladys Halvorsen	Geraldine Fitzgerald
Pop Gruber	Walter Brennan
Toni	Faye Emerson
Doc Ganson	George Coulouris
Al Doyle	George Tobias
Chet King	Robert Shayne
Charles Manning	Richard Gaines
Shake Thomas	James Flavin
Windy Mather	Ralph Peters
Bellboy	Dick Erdman
Priest	William Edmunds
Orchestra leader	Rudy Friml, Jr.
Counter man	Grady Sutton

with

Alex Havier, Ralph Dunn, and John Conte.

Synopsis:

Nick Blake gets out of the army and seeks out his girl, Toni, who is holding fifty thousand dollars of Nick's money. He discovers that Toni has sunk and lost his money in Chet King's nightclub. He forces King to give him the money and, leaving the two-timing Toni, heads for Los Angeles. There he meets an old pal, Pop Gruber. He is also approached by small-time racketeer Doc Ganson with a plan to fleece a rich widow. Although enjoying doing nothing, Nick is finally talked into the deal for a percentage of two-thirds.

Nick begins the swindle by posing as a rich salvage magnate when he meets the young widow, Gladys Halvorsen, and her financial advisor, Manning. Nick pours on the charm, romanticizing Gladys as well as convincing Manning that the salvage business would be a sound investment. While visiting Mission San Juan Capistrano, however, Nick undergoes a change of heart and tells Gladys that he loves her.

Later Doc warns Nick not to back out of the deal. Nick decides to pay off the gangsters with his own money, but in the meantime Manning has learned the truth about Nick's swindle. He tells Gladys, who confronts Nick. Nick refuses to lie, and Gladys tells him she wants and loves him anyway. But Gladys is later kidnapped by Doc, who takes her to an old shack on the waterfront. Nick and his friends Al and Pop trace them and eliminate Doc's gang. Pop kills Doc, but is shot to death himself. Nick and Gladys leave together, remembering Pop's last words: "Don't waste time. Nobody lives forever."

Reviews:
Leonard Maltin in *TV Movies:*
   "Well-done but familiar yarn of con-man Garfield fleecing rich widow Fitzgerald, then falling in love for real."

Bosley Crowther in the *New York Times:*
   "Those customers — of which there are many — who have lived through such matters before are likely to find this repetition just a bit wearisome and even dull . . . . John Garfield and Geraldine Fitzgerald turn in acting jobs which are worthy of better material, and George Tobias is genial and droll as the right-hand man to Mr. Garfield . . . . 'Nobody Lives Forever' proves, indeed, that flesh is weak, we would say."

Notes:
   Nobody Lives Forever had originally been planned for Humphrey Bogart, who refused it.
   Nobody Lives Forever opened at the Strand Theatre in New York on November 1, 1946.

With George Tobias, Robert Shayne.

With George Tobias, Walter Brennan.

With Ralph Peters, George Coulouris, Walter Brennan.

With Geraldine Fitzgerald.

With Geraldine Fitzgerald, Walter Brennan.

26
Humoresque
1947

Credits:

A Warner Bros. Picture. Directed by Jean Negulesco. Produced by Jerry Wald. Screenplay by Clifford Odets and Zachary Gold. Based on a story by Fannie Hurst. Director of photography, Ernest Haller. Music by Franz Waxman. Film editor, Rudi Fehr. Art director, Hugh Reticker. Costumes by Adrian. Orchestrations by Leo F. Forbstein. Music advisor, Isaac Stern. Running time, 125 minutes.

Cast:

Helen Wright	Joan Crawford
Paul Boray	John Garfield
Sid Jeffers	Oscar Levant
Rudy Boray	J. Carroll Naish
Gina	Joan Chandler
Phil Boray	Tom D'Andrea
Florence	Peggy Knudsen
Esther Boray	Ruth Nelson
Monte Loeffler	Craig Stevens
Victor Wright	Paul Cavanaugh
Baver	Richard Gaines
Rozner	John Abbott
Paul, as a child	Bobby Blake
Phil, as a child	Tommy Cook
Eddie	Don McGuire
Hagerstrom	Fritz Leiber
Nightclub singer	Peg LaCentra
Teddy	Richard Walsh

Synopsis:

Ambitious young violinist Paul Boray plays at a party given by Helen Wright, a neurotic society woman. Her husband, Victor, understands the hopelessness of their marriage, and closes his eyes to her unfaithfulness. Helen falls for Paul, mainly because he refuses to be deterred from his dedication to music. She becomes his patron, launching his career and leading him to success. Paul returns her love, but cannot adequately cope with her complexities. Paul's mother disapproves of the affair, even after Helen goes to see her in hopes of bettering the situation. After a quarrel, Helen finds Paul with a former girlfriend and creates a scene. They both come to a final realization that they are totally unsuited in temperament, no matter how great their love. Paul hopes to come to some solution and continue their relationship, but Helen is aware of the hopelessness of their involvement. Listening to Paul play Wagner's *Liebestod,* Helen walks into the ocean and ends the affair.

Reviews:

John McCarten in *The New Yorker:*

"John Garfield, in the role of the violinist, saws away impressively, and Oscar Levant, as a neighborhood pal, plays the piano and makes jokes."

Newsweek:

"If it leaves you a little confused, it isn't the fault of Miss Crawford or Garfield. And if the tragedy of it all proves overpowering, there is always Oscar Levant, who has the best lines in the script and trades each one in for a laugh."

Philip T. Hartung in *Commonweal:*

"John Garfield, as the violinist with the temperament of a genius, is proud, sensitive and intense — but he plays second fiddle to Miss Crawford's interesting and disturbing performance as an alcoholic nymph."

Shirley O'Hara in *The New Republic:*

"The Warner Brothers version showing currently, with Joan Crawford, John Garfield and Oscar Levant, is one of the best movies I've ever seen . . . . John Garfield again manages the touching combination of toughness and sensibility that makes him always interesting to see."

Time:

"Garfield seems as intense and preoccupied as a great genius is commonly reputed to be, and his sullen-deadpan lovemaking might very well, as the plot contends, drive any high-strung lady to speedy self-destruction."

Bosley Crowther in the *New York Times:*

"The music, we must say, is splendid — and, if you will only shut your eyes so that you don't have to watch Mr. Garfield leaning his soulful face against that violin or Miss Crawford violently emoting . . . . you may enjoy it."

Notes:

Humoresque had been filmed once before, in 1920. One of the top-grossing films of 1946-47, the film won one Oscar nomination for Franz Waxman's score, although it lost to *The Best Years of Our Lives'* score by Hugo Friedhofer.

Humoresque opened at the Hollywood Theatre in New York on December 25, 1946.

With Ruth Nelson, J. Carrol Naish.

With Joan Crawford, Paul Cavanaugh.

JOAN CRAWFORD   JOHN GARFIELD

Humoresque

WARNER BROS.

With Joan Crawford.

With Joan Crawford.

With Joan Crawford.

27
Body and Soul
1947

Credits:

An Enterprise Studios production, United Artists release. Directed by Robert Rossen. Produced by Bob Roberts. Screenplay by Abraham Polonsky. Director of photography, James Wong Howe. Music by Rudolph Polk and Hugo Friedhofer. Film editors, Francis Lyon and Robert Parish. Assistant director, Robert Aldrich. Art directors, Nathan Juran and Edward J. Boyle. Costumes by Marion Herward Keyes. Lyrics by Johnny Green, Edward Heyman, Robert Sour, and Frank Eyton. Running time, 104 minutes.

Cast:

Charley Davis	John Garfield
Peg Born	Lili Palmer
Alice	Hazel Brooks
Anna Davis	Anne Revere
Quinn	William Conrad
Shorty Polaski	Joseph Pevney
Ben Chaplin	Canada Lee
Roberts	Lloyd Goff
David Davis	Art Smith
Arnold	James Burke
Irma	Virginia Gregg
Drummer	Peter Virgo
Prince	Joe Devlin
Grocer	Shimin Rushkin
Miss Tedd	Mary Currier
Dan	Milton Kibbie
Shelton	Tim Ryan
Jack Marlowe	Artie Dorrell
Victor	Cy Ring
Marine	Glen Lee
Referee	John Indrisano
Announcer	Dan Tobey
Doctor	Wheaton Chambers

Synopsis:

Charley Davis wins an amateur boxing match and is taken on by promoter Quinn. He also falls in love with Peg, whom he met at the fight. Charley's mother does not want him to fight, but when his father is accidentally killed, Charley sets up a fight for money. He wins this and each successive fight as his career blooms.

Quinn negotiates with unethical promoter Roberts for Charley to fight Ben Chaplin, an old fighter with a brain injury. When Charley KO's Ben, his pal Shorty discovers Ben's old injury and tells off Roberts. Charley, however, sides with Roberts and fires his friend. Shorty is beaten up by Roberts's men and, although rescued by Charley, is killed moments later by a speeding car. When Charley refuses to quit the ring, Peg leaves him.

Charley continues to rise, accompanied by Quinn's old girlfriend, Alice, and Ben Chaplin, whom he hires as his trainer. Peg accepts Charley back when he promises to quit the ring after one more fight, until she learns that he is going to throw the fight. Roberts dumps Ben for trying to talk Charley out of throwing the bout, but Ben's brain injury worsens and he goes wild, collapses, and dies.

Charley goes into the title-defending match against Marlowe, fighting poorly. Late in the fight Charley realizes that Marlowe has been told to hurt him. Charley begins a withering counterattack, finally knocking out Marlowe in a tremendous beating. Facing Roberts, Charley tosses threats aside with, "What are you gonna do, kill me? Everybody dies." With Peg on his arm, he walks back home.

Reviews:
James Agee in *The Nation:*
"It is never as nervy as the best of 'Nightmare Alley,' but of its own kind it is more solidly made.."

John McCarten in *The New Yorker:*
"As the brooding middleweight champion, John Garfield is fairly convincing, except when he tries to ponder the mysteries of the universe between bouts."

Newsweek:
"Garfield, as the fighter, gives a fine portrayal of a hard, arrogant youth who is almost turned into a bum by his desire for money."

Hermine Rich Isaacs in *Theatre Arts:*
"This is Garfield's role, not only from frequent repetion but from birth, and he plays it with a combination of cocky grace and the humorlessness of the self-made man which is more disarming than repugnant."

Time:
"John Garfield, having dropped some of his Dead End mannerisms, gives a good performance that is as hard and simple as a rock."

Bosley Crowther in the *New York Times:*
"John Garfield gives a rattling good performance as the steel-trap fighter . . . . Trim, taut and full of vitality, Mr. Garfield really acts like a fresh kid who thinks the whole world is an easy set-up. Altogether this Enterprise picture . . . hits the all-time high in throat-catching fight films."

Notes:
Body and Soul was a timely release, coming at approximately the same time that New York state was investigating sports "fixing," especially boxing.

Screenwriter Polonsky has said that he fought to keep director Rossen from rewriting the ending. As a substitute for Charley's return to some dignity, as seen, Rossen shot but did not use an ending in which Roberts's men kill Charley, leaving him lying with his head in a garbage can.

One of the top-grossing films of 1947-48, *Body and Soul* won the Academy Award for Best Film Editing. James Wong Howe's cinematography was nominated, but lost to Guy Green's work on *Great Expectations.* Garfield was nominated for Best Actor of the year by both the Academy and the New York Film Critics. He lost the Oscar race to Ronald Colman for *A Double Life,* and the Critics' Award to William Powell for *Life With Father* and *The Senator Was Indiscreet.*

Body and Soul opened at the Globe Theatre in New York on November 9, 1947.

With Virginia Gregg, Lili Palmer.

Garfield and his trainer, John Indrisano.

With Joseph Pevney, Lili Palmer.

With Anne Revere, Joseph Pevney.

28
Gentleman's Agreement
1947

Credits:

A Twentieth Century-Fox production. Directed by Elia Kazan. Produced by Darryl F. Zanuck. Screenplay by Moss Hart. Based on the novel by Laura Z. Hobson. Director of photography, Arthur Miller. Music by Alfred Newman. Film editor, Harman Jones. Art directors, Lyle Wheeler and Mark-Lee Kirk. Running time, 118 minutes.

Cast:

Phil Green	Gregory Peck
Kathy	Dorothy McGuire
Dave	John Garfield
Anne	Celeste Holm
Mrs. Green	Anne Revere
Miss Wales	June Havoc
John Minify	Albert Dekker
Jane	Jane Wyatt
Tommy	Dean Stockwell
Dr. Craigie	Nicholas Joy
Professor Lieberman	Sam Jaffe
Personnel Manager	Harold Vermilyea
Bill Payson	Ransom M. Sherman
Hotel manager	Roy Roberts
Mrs. Minify	Kathleen Lockhart
Bert McAnny	Curt Conway
Bill	John Newland
Weisman	Robert Warwick
Miss Miller	Louise Lorimer
Tingler	Howard Negley
Apartment superintendent	Victor Kilian
Harry	Frank Wilcox
Maitre 'D	Wilton Graff
Clerk	Morgan Farley
Ex-G.I. in restaurant	Robert Karnes
2nd Ex-G.I.	Gene Nelson
Guest	Marion Marshall
Columnist	Mauritz Hugo
1st woman	Olive Deering
2nd woman	Jane Green
3rd woman	Virginia Gregg
Elevator starter	Jesse White

Synopsis:

Writer Phil Green is preparing a series of magazine articles on anti-Semitism, at the same time falling in love with his new publisher's niece, Kathy. Phil decides to pose as a Jew for several weeks in order to learn how it feels. He tells the magazine staff that he is Jewish, beginning the masquerade. Kathy falters, however, when Phil proposes, and wants to tell her family he is not actually a Jew. He then realizes that she is not as liberal as she claims. Phil's Jewish pal, Dave Goldman, returns from the army, and tells Phil how Jews become hardened to anti-Semitism. However, he is not so hardened that he doesn't take a punch at a man in a cafe who calls him a "Yid officer." Dave helps bring Phil and Kathy back together. Upon meeting Kathy's family and friends, though, Phil becomes furious to find that she has screened out all possible Jew-baiters. Phil is won back to a small degree when she rents her house in a "restricted" area to Dave. He continues the articles despite his fears that they will not effect much change.

Reviews:
John McCarten in *The New Yorker:*
  "Among the . . . performers, John Garfield stands out as a Jewish veteran, working up a powerful scene from a simple description of how a Jew in his company of engineers died during the war. He, at least, makes 'Gentleman's Agreement' come alive, if only briefly."

Newsweek:
  "There are two performances which are outstanding. They are given by John Garfield, as a returning Jewish Army officer, and Celeste Holm, as a girl with excellent motives who can't quite get what she wants."

Time:
  "Kazan's sure hand has bottled John Garfield's carbonated talents into a clear, constrained performance as the hero's Jewish friend."

Philip T. Hartung in *Commonweal:*
  "Particularly effective are Gregory Peck as the writer whose irritability with his discoveries are understandable though tiring, John Garfield as his Jewish friend . . . . "

Robert L. Hatch in *The New Republic:*
  "The characters are chosen too consciously as types to advance the argument. It seems overdoing it, for example, that John Garfield, playing Gregory Peck's Jewish boyhood friend, should be an Army captain and thus appear, as it were, wrapped in a flag."

John Mason Brown in *Saturday Review:*
  "There are excellent performances by John Garfield as a returned Jewish veteran, by Anne Revere, and by Celeste Holm."

Bosley Crowther in the *New York Times:*
  "It is this reviewer's opinion that John Garfield's performance of a young Jew, lifelong friend of the hero, is a bit too mechanical. The film still has abundant meaning and should be fully and widely enjoyed."

Notes:
  Gentleman's Agreement was one of the top-grossing films of 1947-48, and it also won many awards. It placed seventh on the National Board of Review's Ten Best list, and was on the *New York Times* and *Film Daily* Ten Best lists. It won the New York Film Critics' Best Picture and Best Director awards. The film took two Best Supporting Actress Oscar nominations, for Anne Revere and Celeste Holm, with Holm winning the award. Gregory Peck was nominated for the Academy's Best Actor award. His performance, however, like Garfield's *Body and Soul* portrayal, lost to Ronald Colman for *A Double Life*. Dorothy McGuire lost the Oscar for Best Actress to Loretta Young for the *The Farmer's Daughter*. Finally, the film won Oscars for Best Director and Best Picture.
  Gentleman's Agreement opened at the Mayfair Theatre in New York on November 11, 1947.

With Dorothy McGuire, Gregory Peck.

With Gregory Peck, Dorothy McGuire, Celeste Holm.

With Dorothy McGuire.

With Gregory Peck.

With Gregory Peck, Celeste Holm, Robert Karnes, Gene
Nelson, players.

29
Force of Evil
1948

Credits:

An Enterprise Studios production, MGM release. Directed by Abraham Polonsky. Produced by Bob Roberts. Screenplay by Abraham Polonsky and Ira Wolfert. Based on the novel *Tucker's People,* by Ira Wolfert. Director of photography, George Barnes. Music by David Raksin. Film editor, Art Seid. Dialogue director, Don Weis. Assistant director, Robert Aldrich. Art director, Richard Day. Set decorations by Edward C. Boyle. Makeup by Gus Norin. Sound recorder, Frank Webster. Orchestrations by Rudolph Polk. Running time, 78 minutes.

Cast:

Joe Morse	John Garfield
Doris Lowry	Beatrice Pearson
Leo Morse	Thomas Gomez
Ben Tucker	Roy Roberts
Edna Tucker	Marie Windsor
Fred Bauer	Howland Chamberlain
Hobe Wheelock	Paul McVey
Juice	Jack Overman
Johnson	Tim Ryan
Mary	Barbara Woodell
Bunty	Raymond Largay
Wally	Stanley Prager
Frankie	Beau Bridges
Badgley	Allan Mathews
Egan	Barry Kelley
Ficco	Paul Fix
Mrs. Morse	Georgia Backus
Two and Two	Sid Tomack
Elevator operator	Paul Frees
Policeman	Richard Reeves
Comptroller	Murray Alper

Synopsis:

Joe Morse, lawyer for Ben Tucker's numbers syndicate, has helped arrange for a fixed lottery on July 4, the one day when superstitious bettors will always bet on 776. That number has been set to win, which will wipe out the small independent numbers banks and allow Tucker to take over. However, Joe's older brother, Leo, runs one of these small banks, and Joe fears that the strain will kill Leo, who has a weak heart. Tucker will not let Joe warn Leo, and Leo will not listen to Joe's subtle hints to sell out before the next day brings ruin. Joe finally resorts to having Leo's bank raided. Leo and his pretty secretary, Doris, are arrested, but still Leo does not get the message. Refusing to welch on bets already placed, Leo is wiped out the next day as 776 comes in. He gives in and becomes a part of Tucker's organization. Joe tries to salvage Doris's job and reputation, help which she refuses although somewhat intrigued by Joe's evil charm. Leo's bookkeeper, Bauer, tries to quit, but Joe warns him that quitting could be dangerous for his health. Bauer decides to inform the police of the banks's locations, hoping that the syndicate will be raided out of existence. He is also approached by gangsters working for Ficco, who wants to muscle in on Tucker's area. Bauer refuses to cooperate.

That evening, Joe is visited by Mrs. Tucker, who warns him that the phones are tapped and then tries to seduce him. Joe gives her the cold shoulder, but is worried about her warning: "A man could spend the rest of his life trying to remember what he shouldn't have said." Joe leaves the office with Doris, who now loves him and who has decided that Joe is Tucker's innocent dupe. Joe loves her, too, but won't lie to her. The next day Leo's bank is raided, and Bauer is arrested along with Leo and the others. A cop thanks Bauer for the tip in front of Leo.

Back at his office, Joe discovers that his law partner, Hobe, is working for the D.A.'s office. Joe cleans out his safe and plans his escape from the mess that is now falling around his ears. Bauer, in the meantime, has set up a meeting between Leo and Ficco, hoping that it will provide his own escape. But Leo is kidnapped by the gang, which murders Bauer when he tries to run. When Joe learns of these developments, he goes to Tucker's office for a showdown. There he learns that Tucker has taken on Ficco as his muscle. Demanding that Ficco release Leo, Joe is told that Leo is dead and has been dumped near the river. Joe surreptitiously takes the bugged phone from the hook while Tucker and Ficco discuss the new business set-up. When Joe threatens to tell all to the police, a three-way shoot-out erupts that leaves Ficco and Tucker dead. Joe and Doris go to the river and find Leo's body. Then Joe slowly turns to go to the police with his confession.

Reviews:
Leonard Maltin in *TV Movies:*
"Excellent study of the numbers racket, with Garfield inexorably involved, battling to break loose."

Bosley Crowther in the *New York Times:*
"This film is a dynamic crime-and-punishment drama, brilliantly and broadly realized. . . . Mr. Polonsky here establishes himself as a man of imagination and unquestioned craftsmanship. True, he was very fortunate in having John Garfield play the young lawyer in the story, for Mr. Garfield is his tough guy to the life. Sentient underneath a steel shell, taut, articulate — he is all good men gone wrong. . . . A sizzling piece of work."

Notes:
Force of Evil was the first film directed by Abraham Polonsky, who had scripted *Body and Soul.* Due to the studio blacklist, Polonsky did not direct again for twenty years. One of his later films was *Tell Them Willie Boy Is Here,* which featured Robert Blake, an actor with the same Garfield tough charm, in a role that Garfield might easily have played. Of *Force of Evil,* Polonsky said, years later, "The hero is about to confess to the police because that is the way we could get a seal."

Force of Evil opened at Loew's State Theatre in New York on December 25, 1948(!).

With Sid Tomack.

With Beatrice Pearson.

With Thomas Gomez.

With Marie Windsor.

With Thomas Gomez.

30
We Were Strangers
1949

Credits:

A Horizon Production, Columbia release. Directed by John Huston. Produced by S. P. Eagle. Associate producer, Jules Buck. Screenplay by Peter Viertel and John Huston. Based on the "China Valdez" episode in Robert Sylvester's novel *Rough Sketch.* Director of photography, Russell Metty. Music by George Antheil. Film editor, Al Clark. Dialogue director, Gladys Hill. Assistant director, Carl Hieke. Art director, Cary Odell. Set decoration by Louis Diage. Costumes by Jean Louis. Hair styles by Larry Germain. Special effects by Lawrence W. Butler. Sound recorder, Lambert Day. Orchestrations by M. W. Stoloff. Running time, 106 minutes.

Cast:

China Valdes	Jennifer Jones
Tony Fenner	John Garfield
Armando Ariete	Pedro Armendariz
Guillermo	Gilbert Roland
Chief	Ramon Novarro
Miguel	Wally Cassell
Ramon	David Bond
Toto	Jose Perez
Bank manager	Morris Ankrum
Manolo	Tito Rinaldo
Roberto	Paul Monte
Bombmaker	Leonard Strong
Rubio	Robert Tafur

160

Synopsis:

When her brother is killed by secret police chief Ariete, China Valdes joins the Cuban underground. She thus meets Tony Fenner, an American fighting with the partisans, but pretending to be searching out Cuban theatrical talent. While walking with China through the cemetery, Tony develops a plan to tunnel under the cemetery to a plot owned by some high official, assassinate him, and blow up the whole Cuban hierarchy at the ensuing state funeral. Tony and China meet with Guillermo, Ramon, and other revolutionaries and begin the tunnel from China's house. One day China is followed home by Ariete, who paws at her, but passes out drunkenly. His servant takes him home, and China becomes hysterical. Tony comforts her and they both realize their mutual love.

With cloth masks, the diggers tunnel through the stench of the cemetery's poor section. Ramon gets sick and delirious, leaves the house, and wanders the streets, babbling about the plot, until he is accidentally run down by a truck. The group reaches the family tomb of their target, whom they then assassinate. However, the bombmaker arrives with the news that the dead man's family has decided to bury him elsewhere. In despair, the foiled plotters beg Tony to escape Cuba. Before he can do so, however, Ariete's men attack. Tony goes down under a hail of machine-gun fire. Crawling to China, he hears church bells signaling the revolt of the populace against their dictators. As Guillermo rushes in to tell of Ariete's death, Tony dies.

Reviews:
Newsweek:
"Garfield, as the masquerading American who is finally exposed as a Cuban exile, gives another of his strong and forthright, if familiar, impersonations."

Robert Hatch in *The New Rupublic:*
"Despite the presence of John Garfield and Jennifer Jones in the leads, 'We Were Strangers' belongs to John Huston, the director. Huston is building himself a reputation as the strongest, most assured director in Hollywood and 'We Were Strangers' is a notably disciplined picture."

Time:
"'Strangers' occasional virtuosity cannot conceal its flaws. Coming from the man who made *The Treasure of Sierra Madre,* it is a disappointment."

Voyeur in *Theatre Arts:*
In our opinion, this is an even better picture than 'Sierra Madre.' Jennifer Jones and John Garfield are excellent, but supporting actors have the juicy roles.'

John McCarten in *The New Yorker:*
"As chief engineer of the cemetery underground, John Garfield is grim, intense, and bold, but also a trifle sticky when he gets to mooning over Miss Jones .... Memorable bit of dialogue: 'Run down to the cellar and get me a bucket of dynamite.'

Bosley Crowther in the *New York Times:*
The cold, calculating perseverance of the young American leader of the group is clinched in the eternal tension of John Garfield in this principal role. And a Cuban laborer with a poet's soul is made by Gilbert Roland into the most genuine and affecting personality in the film. Concentration upon detail and upon the concrete mechanics of the plan has thrown the whole drama into the character of a passionless action film."

Note:
We Were Strangers opened at the Astor Theatre in New York on April 27, 1949.

With Gilbert Roland, Jennifer Jones.

With Jose Perez, David Bond, Ramon Novarro, Wally Cassell, Jennifer Jones, Gilbert Roland.

With Jennifer Jones.

With David Bond, Jose Perez, Jennifer Jones, Gilbert Roland, Wally Cassell.

With Wally Cassell, Jennifer Jones, Gilbert Roland, Jose Perez.

With Wally Cassell, Gilbert Roland, Jennifer Jones.

With Gilbert Roland, David Bond, Jose Perez, Wally Cassell.

31
Jigsaw
(retitled Gun Moll)
1949

Credits:

A Tower Pictures production, United Artists release. Directed by Fletcher Markle. Produced by Edward J. Danziger and Harry Lee Danziger. Screenplay by Fletcher Markle and Vincent McConnor. Based on a story by John Roeburt. Director of photography, Don Malkames. Music by Robert W. Stringer. Film editor, Robert Matthews. Assistnat director, Sal J. Scoppa, Jr. Makeup by Fred Ryle. Special effects by William L. Nemeth. Sound recorder, David M. Polak. Running time, 70 minutes.

Cast:

Howard Malloy	Franchot Tone
Barbara Whitfield	Jean Wallace
Charles Riggs	Myron McCormick
Angelo Agostini	Marc Lawrence
Mrs. Hartley	Winifred Lenihan
Caroline Riggs	Betty Harper
Sigmund Kosterich	Hedley Rainnie
District Attorney Walker	Walter Vaughn
Knuckles	George Breen
Tommy Quigley	Robert Gist
Mrs. Borg	Hester Sondergaard
Pet shop owner	Luella Gear
Pemberton	Alexander Campbell
Waldron	Robert Noe
Nichols	Alexander Lockwood
Wylie	Ken Smith
Museum guard	Alan Macateer
Warehouse guard	Manuel Aparicio
Butler	Brainard Duffield

Unbilled guests

Woman in nightclub	Marlene Dietrich
Man in nightclub	Fletcher Markle
Waiter	Henry Fonda
Loafer	John Garfield
Secretary	Marsha Hunt
Columnist	Leonard Lyons
Bartender	Burgess Meredith

Synopsis:

Assistant District Attorney Howard Malloy is investigating a series of murders, including that of crusading newspaperman Charles Riggs. In the course of his work, Malloy uncovers an evil antireligious racist hate-group that includes political crook Angelo Agostini and a gunman named Knuckles. Malloy tracks down the group and confronts them finally in a Modern Art museum.

164

Variety:

"Carrying on the cinematic attack against race and religious intolerance, *Jigsaw* is a well-intentioned but lightweight film."

Bosley Crowther in the *New York Times:*

"On the sole account of 'Jigsaw,' Hollywood has no reason to look immediately to its laurels. John Garfield is seen as a loafer, Henry Fonda as a waiter in a club, Burgess Meredith as a bartender, Marsha Hunt as a secretary and such. This tomfooling doesn't help the picture.

Notes:

Garfield was doing *The Big Knife* on Broadway when he did this guest stint as a favor to Franchot Tone. Henry Fonda took a minute away from *Mr. Roberts* to do the same thing.

Jigsaw was renamed *Gun Moll* when sold to television, in order to avoid confusion with a TV series of the same name.

Jigsaw opened at the Mayfair Theatre in New York on May 29, 1949.

32
Under My Skin
1950

Credits:

A Twentieth Century-Fox production. Directed by Jean Negulesco. Produced by Casey Robinson. Screenplay by Casey Robinson. Based on the story "My Old Man," by Ernest Hemingway. Director of photography, Joseph La Shelle. Music by Daniele Amfitheatrof. Film editor, Dorothy Spencer. Art directors, Lyle Wheeler and Maurice Ransford. Set decoration by Thomas Little and Walter M. Scott. Costumes by Charles Le Maire. Makeup by Ben Nye. Special effects by Fred Sersen. Sound recorders, George Leverett and Harry M. Leonard. Orchestrations by Maurice de Packh and Earle Hagen. Songs by Alfred Newman and Jacques Surmagne. Running time, 86 minutes.

Cast:

Dan Butler	John Garfield
Paule Manet	Micheline Prelle
Louis Bork	Luther Adler
Joe	Orley Lindgren
George Gardner	Noel Drayton
Maurice	A. A. Merola
Rico	Ott George
Max	Paul Bryar
Henriette	Ann Codee
Bartender	Steve Geray
Rigoli	Joseph Warfield
Doctor	Eugene Borden
Nurse	Loulette Sablon
Detective	Alphonse Martell
Hotel clerk	Ernesto Morelli
Express man	Jean Del Val
Attendant	Hans Herbert
Flower woman	Esther Zeitlin
Doorman	Maurice Brierre
Barman	Gordon Clark
Official	Frank Arnold
American mother	Elizabeth Flournoy
Italian officer	Mario Siletti
Porter	Guy Zanette
Gendarme	Andre Charise
Drake	Harry Martin
Girl in Cafe	Dusty Anderson Negulesco

Synopsis:

Veteran jockey Dan Butler wins a steeplechase race in Italy, although he had arranged to throw it for racketeer Louis Bork. That night Bork's men rough up Dan, but the police arrive in time to prevent any real harm. Some days later, Dan and his young son, Joe, arrive in Paris to look up an old friend of Dan's. The friend, they learn, has died, but they meet his young widow, Paule. She tells Dan that her husband was killed because of the trouble Dan had brought him, and she asks him to leave. A few days pass, and Dan encounters Bork again. The crook tells Dan that he is still waiting for the money owed him on the race Dan failed to throw in Italy. Dan promises to get it as soon as he can. Sick with worry, Dan confides in Paule, who has managed to fall in love with him. Dan rides in another fixed race, and Joe sees him sneaking up to collect his winnings, When he confronts his father, Dan decides to send the boy back to America. But Joe cannot bear to leave even though he knows of his father's cheating. Dan decides to take Paule and Joe to the U.S. after one last race. However, Bork insists that Dan throw this one as well. Dan gets a friend, jockey George Gardner, to guard him from any horses Bork might send in to block him, but George's horse goes down in an attempt to protect Dan. Dan races for the finish line, winning strongly, but he crashes into George's riderless mount and is killed. Paule takes Joe back home to America.

Reviews:

Jane Lockhart in *The Rotarian:*

"Many scenes and characterizations are ambiguous. On the whole, the film holds your interest, and its plot is off the beaten track."

John McCarten in *The New Yorker:*

"Mr. Garfield plays the jockey as if he'd been born in a tack room .... Negulesco has kept things going at a hell of a clip."

Robert Hatch in *The New Republic:*

"The movie is a sentimental tearjerker, a kind of literature to which Hemingway is not addicted."

Newsweek:

"When left to themselves Garfield and Lindgren are every bit the father and son Hemingway intended."

New York Times:

"We're afraid that Mr. Robinson, who wrote and produced the film, has expanded the Hemingway story into a characterization and meaningless romance. The jockey, played by John Garfield, is a bumptious and brutish sort of a chap .... A limp and pallid affair."

Notes:

Studio accountant Albert Valentino, brother of Rudolph Valentino, helped Garfield with his Italian lines in this film.

Under My Skin opened at the Roxy Theatre in New York on March 17, 1950.

With Orley Lindgren.

With Orley Lindgren, Noel Drayton.

168

With Micheline Prelle.

With Orley Lindgren.

169

With Orley Lindgren, Micheline Prelle.

With Noel Drayton.

33
Difficult Years
(Anni difficili)
1950

Credits:

A Briguglio Films production, Lopert Films release. Directed by Luigi Zampa. Produced by Falco Laudati. Screenplay by Sergio Amidei, Vitaliano Brancati, Franco Evangelisti, and Enrico Fulchignono. Based on the novel by Vitaliano Brancati. English narrative by Arthur Miller. Director of photography, Carlo Montevori. Music by Franco Casavola. Running time, 90 minutes.

Cast:

Aldo Piscitello	Umberto Spadaro
Giovanni	Massimo Girotti
Rosina	Ave Ninchi
Elena	Odette Bedogni
Grandpa	Ernesto Almirante
The twins	Di Stefano Brothers
Maria	Milly Vitale
The baron	Enzo Biliotti
The baron's son	Carletto Sposito
The Fascist minister	Loris Gizzi
The pharmacist	Aldo Silvani
The American	Turi
Narrator	John Garfield

Synopsis:

Aldo Piscitello, a minor government clerk in a small Sicilian town, is told in 1934 to join the Fascist party or face dismissal. His intellectual friends sympathize with him in the rear of the town pharmacy, but he submits to his wife's persuasion and begins attending meetings and drill sessions. His son in the army, Giovanni, becomes engaged to the pharmacist's daughter, but is ordered to Ethiopia. He later marries her, then fights in Spain while his father and friends ineffectually talk against Mussolini. When France is invaded, the pharmacist walks through a crowd, singing "La Marseillaise" and is imprisoned. The son is killed by Germans while returning home, and the father is ironically discharged as an old-line Fascist upon American liberation of the town.

Reviews:

Voyeur in *Theatre Arts:*

"Miller's prologue, portentously narrated by John Garfield, is valid in that it sets the stage historically for what we are about to see dramatized."

Robert Hatch in *The New Republic:*

"It is a tedious, over-simplified, predictable account of how Mussolini's total state destroyed one of its most inoffensive citizens."

Philip Hamburger in *The New Yorker:*

"Arthur Miller has not helped matters by contributing some windy passages in English, which are narrated by John Garfield in a peculiarly hesitant manner."

Time:

"In some scenes the movie's soundtrack carries an unnecessary commentary written by Playwright Arthur Miller and spoken by John Garfield; the best that can be said for it is that it is inoffensive."

Merle Miller in *The Saturday Review:*

"Arthur Miller's subtitles are frequently preten-

tious, and John Garfield's narration occasionally interfered with the otherwise wonderfully sustained mood. 'Difficult Years' is an important movie. It has something to say not only about Italy during the fascist years but about all of us."

New York Times:

"An English commentary by Arthur Miller, which John Garfield now and then speaks, contributes no more to understanding than do the English subtitles for the dialogue."

Notes:

Garfield and playwright Miller saw the Italian version of *Difficult Years* in Rome in 1948. Impressed, they arranged with Lopert Pictures to work on an American translation.

Difficult Years opened at the World Theatre in New York on August 21, 1950.

Massimo Girotti, Umberto Spadaro.

Loris Gizzi, Umberto Spadaro.

174

34
The Breaking Point
1950

Credits:

A Warner Bros.-First National Picture. Directed by Michael Curtiz. Produced by Jerry Wald. Screenplay by Ranald McDougall. Based on "To Have and Have Not," by Ernest Hemingway. Director of photography, Ted McCord. Film editor, Alan Crosland, Jr. Dialogue director, Edward Carrere. Set decoration by George James Hopkins. Costumes by Leah Rhodes. Sound recorder, Leslie G. Hewitt. Orchestrations by Ray Heindorf. Second unit director, David C. Gardner. Running time, 97 minutes.

Cast:

Harry Morgan	John Garfield
Leona Charles	Patricia Neal
Lucy Morgan	Phyllis Thaxter
Wesley Park	Juano Hernandez
Duncan	Wallace Ford
Rogers	Edmon Ryan
Hannagan	Ralph Dumke
Danny	Guy Thompson
Concho	William Campbell
Amelia	Sherry Jackson
Connie	Donna Jo Boyce
Mr. Sing	Victor Sen Yung
Macho	Peter Brocco
Gotch	John Doucette
Charlie	James Griffith
Dock attendant	Norman Fields
Joseph	Juan Hernandez

Synopsis:

Fishing boat captain Harry Morgan charters his boat to Hannagan and Hannagan's kept woman, Leona Charles, for a trip to Mexico. Morgan is attracted to Leona, although he has a wife, Lucy, and two daughters. After the trip, Morgan finds himself without funds and so agrees to smuggle eight illegal Chinese into the U.S. for a Mr. Sing. Morgan is forced to kill him and set the Chinese ashore. When the refugees are found later, the Coast Guard suspects Morgan and impounds his boat. Crooked lawyer Duncan, however, obtains its release in order for Morgan to transport four criminals, Concho, Danny, Macho, and Gotch, to pick up stolen racetrack receipts. On the way, Morgan's partner, Wesley Park, is killed by the hoods, and he learns that they have the same plans in store for him. One by one, Morgan stalks and kills the criminals, but he is wounded and eventually loses an arm. He recovers and returns to a lawful life with Lucy.

Reviews:

William Pfaff in *Commonweal:*

"Garfield gives an extremely good performance as a man who has made out for himself all his life;

175

finding out in the end the price of having others than himself to make out for."

John McCarten in *The New Yorker:*
"As the boatman, John Garfield is excellent, and he gets fine support from the others in the cast. Michael Curtiz is to be commended for his direction."

Time:
"An expert piece of hard-boiled cinema. In his meatiest role in years, Actor Garfield gives one of his best performances."

Newsweek:
"There is a good deal of eminently satisfactory blood and thunder mixed up in Garfield's losing battle, but neither he nor Miss Neal gives much warmth or depth to a hopelessly star-crossed pair."

Bosley Crowther in the *New York Times:*
"John Garfield is tops in the principal role . . . .

What we have here is a good, taut adventure story . . . . Mr. Garfield is a big help in this respect — his playing of Harry Morgan is the shrewdest, hardest acting in the show."

Notes:
Hemingway's story "To Have and Have Not" was also used as a basis for parts of two other Warner pictures, *To Have and Have Not* and *Key Largo.* The Breaking Point was the only one to stick closely to the original story line, although the locale was switched from Florida to California. The Florida location was retained in the 1958 remake with Audie Murphy, *The Gun Runners.* Garfield was quoted as saying, "I think it's the best I've done since *Body and Soul.* Better than that." Juano Hernandez's son in the film was played by his real son, Juan.

The Breaking Point opened at the Strand Theatre in New York on October 6, 1950.

With Phyllis Thaxter, Sherry Jackson, Donna Jo Boyce.

With Patricial Neal, Juano Hernandez.

With Peter Brocco, Wallace Ford, Guy Thompson, William Campbell.

With Guy Thompson, William Campbell.

With Juano Hernandez.

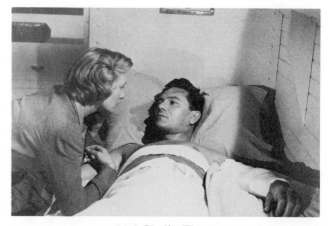

With Phyllis Thaxter.

178

35
He Ran All the Way
1951

Credits:

A United Artist release of an Enterprise production. Directed by John Berry. Produced by Bob Roberts. Associate producer, Paul Trivers. Screenplay by Hugo Butler and Guy Endore. Based on the novel by Sam Ross. Director of photography, James Wong Howe. Music by Franz Waxman. Film editor, Francis D. Lyon. Assistant director, Emmett Emerson. Art director, Harry Horner. Running time, 77 minutes.

Cast:

Nick	John Garfield
Peg	Shelley Winters
Mr. Dobbs	Wallace Ford
Mrs. Dobbs	Selena Royle
Mrs. Robey	Gladys George
Al Molin	Norman Lloyd
Tommy Dobbs	Bobby Hyatt
Stan	Clancy Cooper

Synopsis:

Nick and his partner, Al Molin, kill a policeman during a payroll holdup. Al is killed and Nick hides in a public pool where he meets Peg Dobbs. He accompanies her to the small apartment where she lives with her family. He terrorizes her parents who are forced to let him live with them. Peg falls in love with Nick and goes out to buy an automobile so he can escape with her. Her father hears of this and rushes out. The automobile is late in being delivered, so Nick, who does not trust Peg, forces her at gunpoint to leave with him. Outside is Mr. Dobbs, who shoots Nick's revolver from his hand. Peg picks it up and shoots Nick to death as the car arrives.

Reviews:

Robert Hatch in *The New Rupublic*

"Not as much was made of the possibilities in 'He Ran All the Way' as could have been and, with John Garfield and Shelley Winters in the leads, certainly should have been. The picture skims the surface."

Philip T. Hartung in *Commonweal:*

"Garfield has played the unhappy, chip-on-the-shoulder young man many times before, but this time when he loses his partner, he's more confused than ever. Actually 'He Ran All the Way' is a pretty good thriller."

Bosley Crowther in the *New York Times:*

"John Garfield's stark performance of the fugitive who desperately contrives to save himself briefly from capture is full of startling glints from start to end. He makes a most odd and troubled creature . . . . And in Mr. Garfield's performance, vis-a-vis the rest of the cast, is conveyed a small measure of the irony and the pity that was in the book. All in all, there is shock and grim excitement in this studiously horrifying film, but it soon assumes the look of sheer theatrics when it lays its assumptions on the line."

Notes:

Director John Berry and co-scripter Hugo Butler's names were removed from the credits for a time after release, due to alleged connections with the Communist Party. This explains Emmett Emerson, the assistant director, occasionally being credited with the direction of the picture.

He Ran All the Way, which Garfield co-produced, was his last film. He had plans to follow it with *The Man With the Golden Arm,* but censorship problems, the Congressional hearings, and, in Shakespeare's words, "death, untimely death," prevented this project. We were to have no more keepsakes.

He Ran All The Way opened at the Paramount Theatre in New York on June 20, 1951.

With Gladys George.

With Norman Lloyd.

With Shelley Winters, Bobby Hyatt, Wallace Ford.

With Bobby Hyatt, Shelley Winters, Wallace Ford, Selena Royle.

With Wallace Ford, Shelley Winters, players.

Appendix I
Garfield and Footlight Parade

For many years it has been generally accepted that John Garfield made a brief appearance as an extra in Busby Berkeley's 1933 musical *Footlight Parade.* This belief was fostered by the fact that someone looking incredibly like Garfield is briefly seen during the "Shanghai Lil" brawl scene, and nourished by the fact that Garfield was in California at the time the film was made. The Garfield question aside, *Footlight Parade* was not made in New York, as some recent biographers have stated.

Ed Medard, in researching the details of this supposed appearance, interviewed Berkeley dancers, extras, the still photographer on the film, as well as examining studio employment records and the film itself. He determined that Garfield was not in the film, and even met a dancer who knew the actual extra, a bit player who is now dead.

In attaining frame blow-ups of the sequence (which lasts less than one second on screen), the author discovered the truly astonishing resemblance of the extra to Garfield. However, microscopic examination of the blow-ups reveals that the extra's ears, an excellent means of indentification, are set lower on the head than Garfield's. What is more significant is the fact that the ears are shaped considerably differently than Garfield's, which were much fleshier in the lobe. Other minute differences such as jaw shape, hair type, and the naso-labial area indicate that, though the likeness is startling, it is nothing more than a likeness. John Garfield is not in *Footlight Parade.*

The accompanying photographs are actual frame enlargements, comprising the entire sequence. On screen it lasts 5/6 of one second. The dark areas on the extra's face are smudges of make-up. My thanks go to John Wooley for supplying the film print, and to Dennis Fry for making the enlargements and supplying other photographic services.

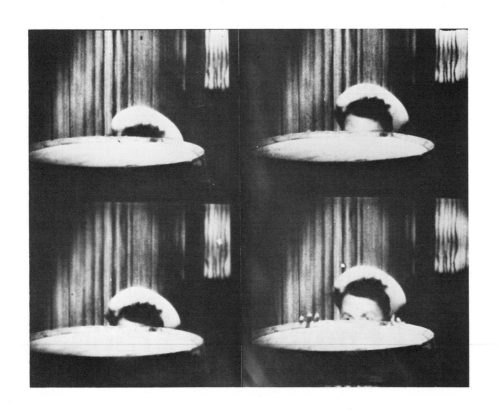

Appendix II
Notes on the Stage Plays

Aside from working as an entertainer at Camp Milford, Connecticut, and other Borscht Belt summer camps, John Garfield made seventeen professional theater appearances. The following list also excludes benefits and USO productions during the war.

Lost Boy, by T.C. Upham. Produced by Burton Harford at the Mansfield Theatre in New York. Opened on January 5, 1932, running for fifteen performances. Jules Garfield played "Bill" in a cast that included Elisha Cook, Jr. in the lead.

Counsellor-at-Law, by Elmer Rice. Produced by the Civic Repertory Theatre group simultaneously in Chicago and New York. Jules Garfield played a messenger for a short time in Chicago, then opened in New York in early 1932, at the Plymouth Theatre. Garfield played Henry Susskind in a cast that included Paul Muni, John Qualen, and Ned Glass. The play ran for a total of 120 performances.

Peace On Earth, by George Sklar and Albert Maltz. Produced by the Theatre Union at the Civic Repertory Theatre. Opened on November 29, for 126 performances, with Jules Garfield in the role of the messenger. Reopened on March 31, 1934, at the 44th Street Theatre, for eighteen performances, with Garfield in dual roles as the messenger and "Bob Peters."

Gold Eagle Guy, by Melvin Levy. Produced by the Group Theatre and D.A. Doran, Jr. at the Morosco Theatre. Opened on November 28, 1934, with Jules Garfield in dual roles as a sailor and "Mackay," in a cast that

Jules Garfinkle (right) in the Heckscher Foundation production of A Midsummer Night's Dream, *c. 1930.*

In Counsellor-at-Law, *1932.*

With Luther Adler, Art Smith in Awake and Sing, *1935.*

included Clifford Odets, Elia Kazan, and Morris Carnovsky. Closed after sixty-five performances.

Waiting For Lefty, by Clifford Odets. Produced by the Group Theatre at the Civic Repertory Theatre. Opened on February 10, 1935, with Jules Garfield in the role of "Sid."

Awake and Sing, By Clifford Odets. Produced by the Group Theatre at the Belasco Theatre. Opened on February 19, 1935 for 185 performances, with Jules Garfield in the role of "Ralph Berger." Cast included Art Smith, Stella Adler, and Roman Bohnen. Reopened on September 9, 1935 for twenty-four performances. *New York Times:* "Jules Garfield plays the part with a splendid sense of character development."

Weep For the Virgins, by Nellise Child. Produced by the Group Theatre at the 46th Street Theatre. Opened on November 30, 1935, for nine performances. Jules Garfield played "Hap Nichols" in a cast that included Evelyn Varden, Art Smith, and J. Edward Bromberg.

The Case of Clyde Griffiths. Opened on March 13, 1936, at the Ethel Barrymore Theatre. Jules Garfield played a workingman.

Johnny Johnson, by Paul Green and Kurt Weill. Produced by the Group Theatre at the 44th Street Theatre. Opened on November 19, 1936, for sixty-eight performances. Jules Garfield played "Johann Lang" in a cast that included Lee J. Cobb, Elia Kazan, and Russell Collins.

Having Wonderful Time, by Arthur Kober. Produced by Marc Connelly with Bela Blau at the Lyceum Theatre. Opened on February 20, 1937, for 132 performances. Jules Garfield played "Chick Kessler" in a cast that included Cornel Wilde, Herb Vigran, and Robert Strauss. *New York Herald-Tribune:* "Jules Garfield has the sort of perception that makes an admirable character of Chick Kessler and he knows how to convey them in the theatre."

Golden Boy, by Clifford Odets. Produced by the Group

With Ruth Nelson in Weep For the Virgins, *1935.*

With Morris Carnovsky in Golden Boy, *1937.*

With Sydney Fox in Having Wonderful Time, *1937.*

With Aline MacMahon in The Heavenly Express, *1940.*

Theatre at the Belasco Theatre. Opened on November 4, 1937, for 250 performances. Jules Garfield played "Siggie" in a cast that included Luther Adler and Lee J. Cobb. *London Observer:* " 'Golden Boy' offered some of the best character acting that I saw in New York, notably Jules Garfield and Morris Carnovsky."

Heavenly Express, by Albert Bein. Produced by Kermit Bloomgarden at the National Theatre. Opened on April 18, 1940, for twenty performances. John Garfield played "The Overland Kid" in a cast that included Harry Carey and Jack Lambert. *New York Daily News:* "Young Mr. Garfield's Overland Kid is alive with enthusiasm and a complete belief in his author and himself."

Awake and Sing, by Clifford Odets. Produced by the Actors Laboratory at the Laboratory Theatre in Hollywood. Opened in June 1946. John Garfield played the role originally performed by Luther Adler. Alfred Ryder played Garfield's former role.

Skipper Next to God, by Jan de Hartog. Produced by the Experimental Theatre at the Maxine Elliott Theatre. Opened on January 4, 1948, for four performances. Reopened on January 29, for ninety-three performances, at the Playhouse Theatre. John Garfield played Capt. Joris Kuiper, and won an Antoinette Perry Award. *New*

In Skipper Next to God, *1948.*

York Herald-Tribune: "Mr. Garfield fills the whole performance with vitality by the force, directness and perception of his acting .... Mr. Garfield is a fiery ... uncommonly enlightened actor."

The Big Knife, by Clifford Odets. Produced by Dwight Deere Wiman at the National Theatre. Opened on

With Nancy Kelly in The Big Knife, *1949.*

With Mildred Dunnock in the ANTA production of Peer Gynt, *1951. (Photo courtesy of the Hoblitzelle Theatre Collection, Humanities Research Center, University of Texas at Austin.)*

February 24, 1949, for 108 performances. John Garfield played "Charlie Castle" in a cast that included Nancy Kelly and J. Edward Bromberg. *New York Sun:* "John Garfield, with his intense and resourceful playing, does more for the character . . . than the author did."

Peer Gynt, by Henrik Ibsen, adapted by Paul Green. Produced by Cheryl Crawford and R.L. Stevens at the ANTA Playhouse. Opened on January 28, 1951, for thirty-two performances. John Garfield played the title role in a cast that included Karl Malden. *New York Daily News:* "Mr. Garfield is an admirable and likeable realistic actor. But his performance is literal and casual, and is completely lacking in poetic animation."

Golden Boy, by Clifford Odets. Produced by ANTA at the ANTA Playhouse. Opened on March 12, 1952, for fifty-five performances. John Garfield, in his final role, played Joe Bonaparte in a cast that included Lee J. Cobb, Jack Warden, and Jack Klugman. *New York World-Telegram:* "As the prizefighter, Mr. Garfield is giving one of his most eloquent performances, purged of the overeager mannerisms that used to mar his acting. Apart from its fervor, his acting now is candid and forceful and more fluent than the part."

With Art Smith in the Golden Boy *revival, 1952.*

Appendix III
John Garfield's Radio Appearances

"Silver Theatre" — CBS — February 12, 1939.

"Silver Theatre" — CBS — February 19, 1939.

"Lux Radio Theatre" — *"Four Daughters"* — CBS — with Priscilla, Lola, Rosemary, and Leota Lane. December 18, 1939.

"Lux Radio Theatre" — *Pinocchio* — CBS — December 25, 1939.

"Lux Radio Theatre" — *Dust Be My Destiny* — CBS — with Claire Trevor. April 14, 1941.

"Free World Radio" — *Tomorrow* — with Beulah Bondi, written by Budd Schulberg and Jerome Lawrence, produced and directed by Arch Oboler. Broadcast during the war years.

"Free World Radio" — *The Second Battle of Warsaw* — with Alan Baxter, written by Irving Ravetch, produced and directed by Arch Oboler. Broadcast during the war years.

"Lux Radio Theatre" — *Pride of the Marines* — CBS — with Eleanor Parker and Dane Clark. December 31, 1945.

"Lux Radio Theatre" — *Body and Soul* — CBS — with Jane Wyman and Marie Windsor. November 15, 1948.

This list includes only dramatic radio appearances and excludes guest appearances on comedy and variety programs.

Appendix IV
A Letter from a Friend

From the New York Times, *May 25, 1952.*
To the drama editor:

The use of your valuable space is asked to say a few words about the gifted John Garfield, star of the American stage and screen, and his untimely death last week, so stunning to all of his admirers and friends.

These past two years he was tired, no doubt. He had had his share of career troubles — financial projects gone wrong, witch-hunters searching his closets, attacks in part of the press for alleged impolitic activities, and sometimes bad health to boot. But Garfield's abundant and energetic nature did not flag in its outpouring of plans and work.

He had finished only recently a not unsuccessful ANTA revival of "Golden Boy, " the third play he had done for that high-minded organization: "Skipper Next to God" and "Peer Gynt," in an adaptation by Paul Green, being the previous productions to which Garfield had generously donated his valued services. His next plans were to join Franchot Tone for a few weeks of summer stock in Florida and to help produce, later in the year, a first play by Norman Brooks, a new and talented writer. After this would have come my play-in-work, "By the Sea."

In these keen and bitter times, highly placed and so open to any wild attacks, Garfield remained extraordinarily free of malice and meanness — they were nowhere in his nature. Despite any and all gossip to the contrary, I, who was in a position to know, state without equivocation that of all his possessions Garfield was proudest of his American heritage, even rudely so. In all ways he was as pure an American product as can be seen these days, processed by democracy, knowing or caring nothing for any other culture or race.

His climb from bare poverty to stardom illustrated for him one of the most cherished folkways of our people. His feelings never changed that he had been mandated by the American people to go in and "keep punching" for them. His success, as he felt it, was the common property of millions, not peculiarly his own. This, I submit, was a basic purity of which not even Garfield himself was conscious.

Few actors on our stage throw themselves into their work with the zest displayed by Garfield; only those who had not known him before would be surprised by his rehearsal period humility. Affectionate by nature, charming and often refreshingly candid, he mostly reserved for friends a glimpse of something true and precious — the ardor of a boy for learning and growth.

Many believed, and among them such critics as Brooks Atkinson and Richard Watts, Jr. in their last reviews, that John Garfield at thirty-nine was just beginning to reveal himself as an actor in terms of wider range, new sensitivity, and maturity. They were correct, for the sheen of Hollywood fooled him only a little; and one may surmise that in his work he felt himself a beginner, while in his life he had come to know himself as a man seeking his identity.

I ask, finally, to be permitted to forget the present hushed austerities and say simply, "Julie, dear friend, I will always love you."

New York, N.Y.

Clifford Odets

Index

Page numbers set in bold type refer to illustrations.

Kazan, Elia, 22, 42, 152, 153, 189
Keef, Candy. *See* Monday, Candy
Kellaway, Cecil, **31**, 136, 138
Kelley, Barry, 156
Kelly, Nancy, **192**
Kelsey, Fred, 118
Kennedy, Arthur, 108
Kennedy, Bill, 119, 129
Kennedy, Jay, 43
Kennedy, Tom, 84
Kent, Arnold, 117
Kentucky, 50
Kern, James V., 117
Kerr, Donald, 49
Keyes, Marion Herward, 148
Key Largo, 176
Kibbie, Milton, 148
Killian, Victor, 69, 152
Killifer, Jack, 53
King, Andrea, 128
King, Dennis, 124
Kingsford, Walter, 61
Kirk, Mark-Lee, 112, 152
Kissel, William, 69
Klugman, Jack, 42, 192
Knox, Alexander, 92, **93**
Knudsen, Peggy, 144
Kober, Arthur, 22, 189
Koenekamp, H. F., 92, 108, 117
Korngold, Erich Wolfgang, 61, 92, 124
Kruger, Otto, 21
Kuhn, Mickey, 61
Kuter, Leo, 117, 119, 128
Kuzelle, Dudley, 118
Kyser, Kay, 116

LaCentra, Peg, 144
Lackteen, Frank, 61, 92
Laemmle, Carl, **24**
La Guardia Award, The, 34
Laidlaw, Ethan, 92
Lamarr, Hedy, 103, 104, **107**, 116
Lambert, Jack, 26, 191
Lamour, Dorothy, 116
Landa, Mary, 117, 119
Landis, Carole, 116
Lane, Leota, 194
Lane, Lola, 49, 65, **66**, 73, **74**, 194
Lane, Priscilla, 26, 49, **50**, **52**, 65, **66**, **67**, **68**, 69, **70**, **71**, **72**, 73, **74**, 194
Lane, Richard, 108, 117
Lane, Rosemary, **26**, 49, 57, **60**, 65, **66** 73, **74**, 194
Langton, Paul, 119
Lardner, David, 109, 113, 120
Lardner, Ring, Jr., 32
Largay, Raymond, 156
LaRue, Jack, 88, **91**
La Shelle, Joseph, 166
"Late John Garfield Blues, The," 15
Laudati, Falco, 172
Laughton, Charles, 19, 32
Laurel, Stan, 30
Lawes, Lewis E., 76
Lawrence, Gertrude, 116
Lawrence, Jerome, 194

Lawrence, Marc, 69, 164
Lawson, John Howard, 33
"Leave It To Beaver" (television series), 113
Leavitt, Al, 30
Lederer, Francis, **27**
Lee, Canada, 148
Lee, Glen, 148
Lee, Robert B., 69, 76, 119
Leftwich, Alexander, 61
Le Gallienne, Eva, 21
Le Maire, Charles, 166
Lenihan, Winifred, 164
Leonard, Harry M., 166
Leonard, Sheldon, 103, **105**, **107**
Leslie, Joan, 117, 128, **131**
Lesser, Sol, 129
Levant, Oscar, 144, 145
Leverett, George, 166
Levy, Melvin, 22, 187
Lewis, Vera, 49, 57, 73
Lieber, Fritz, 21, 144
Life of Emile Zola, The, 62
Life of Jimmy Dolan, The, 54
Life with Father, 149
Lindgren, Orley, 166, **167**, **168**, **169**, **170**
Litel, John, 69, 76
Little, Thomas, 166
Litvak, Anatole, 76, 96, 97, 116
Lloyd, George, 119
Lloyd, Norman, 179, **181**
Lockhart, Gene, 92, **93**
Lockhart, Jane, 167
Lockhart, Kathleen, 152
Lockwood, Alexander, 164
Loesser, Frank, 103, 117
Lombard, Carole, 116
London, Jack, 29, 92, 93
London Observer, The, 191
Look, 34
Look Homeward Angel, 32
Lopert Films, 172, 173
Lorimer, Louise, 152
Lorre, Peter, 34, 128
Lost Boy, 21, 187
Louis, Jean, 160
Love, Montagu, 61
Low, Warren, 61, 69, 96
Loy, Myrna, **24**, 116
Lucas, Wilfrid, 92
Luker, Art, 119, 128
Lundigan, William, 88, 91
Lunt, Alfred, 116
Lupino, Ida, 92, **93**, **94**, **95**, 96, **98**, 118, 128
"Lux Radio Theatre," 194
Lyles, Lee, **26**
Lynn, Jeffrey, 49, 65, 73
Lyon, Francis D., 148, 179
Lyons, Leonard, 164
Lys, Lya, **26**

Macateer, Alan, 164
Macauley, Richard, 96
McCarten, John, 137, 144, 149, 153, 161, 167, 176

McColm, Ralph, 119
McConaghy, Jack, 124
McConnor, Vincent, 164
McCord, Ted, 175
McCormick, Myron, 164
McCracken, Joan, 129
McDaniel, Hattie, 117
McDaniel, Sam, 53
McDonald, Francis, 92
McDougall, Ronald, 175
McEvoy, Fred, 118
McGann, William, 57, 140
McGuire, Don, 132, 144
McGuire, Dorothy, 152, **153**, **154**
McHugh, Frank, **26**, 49, 65, **66**, 69, 73
McHugh, Matt, 117
MacKenna's Gold, 29
MacKenzie, Aeneas, 61
MacMahon, Aline, **24**, 26, 96, **191**
MacMullan, Hugh, 84, 88
MacMurray, Fred, 116
McQueen, Steve, 43
McVey, Paul, 156
Macy's (department store), 22
Madison House, 34
Mahin, John Lee, 103
Malatesta, Fred, 61
Malden, Karl, 37, 192
Malkames, Don, 164
Mallinson, Rory, 132, **134**
Malone, Dorothy, 129
Maltese Falcon, The, 113
Maltin, Leonard, 89, 141, 157
Maltz, Albert, 22, 32, 119, 120, 132, 133, 187
Manhattan Melodrama, 77, 89
Mann, Hank, 117
Manning, Irene, 129
Mantle, Burns, 22, 26
Mantz, Paul, 108
Man with the Golden Arm, The, 50, 180
Marcelle, Lou, 119
March, Fredric, 34
March of Time, The, 116
Markle, Fletcher, 34, 164
Marks, Owen, 80, 132
Marley, Peverall, 132
Marr, Eddie, 128
Marshall, Brenda, 88, **90**, **91**
Marshall, Charles, 108
Marshall, Marion, 152
Marshall, William, 84, 88
Martell, Alphonse, 166
Martin, Harry, 166
Martin, Nora, 129
Marx, Chico, 30
Marx, Groucho, 24
Mason, Louis, 92, **94**
Massey, Raymond, 99, **101**, **102**
Mathews, Allan, 156
Matthews, Lester, 124
Matthews, Robert, 164
Mattis, Jack, 128
Mature, Victor, 116
Maybe It's Love, 81
Mayfair, Mitzi, 30, 116
Mayo, Frank, 84, 136